Religion vs. Television

Religion vs. Television

Competitors in Cultural Context

JAY NEWMAN

Media and Society Series

Westport, Connecticut
London

Library of Congress Cataloging-in-Publication Data

Newman, Jay.
    Religion vs. television : competitors in cultural context / Jay
Newman.
        p. cm.—(Media and society series, ISSN 0890–7161)
      Includes bibliographical references and index.
      ISBN 0–275–95640–7 (alk. paper)
      1. Television in religion. I. Title. II. Series.
    BV656.3.N38   1996
    291.1'75—dc20   96–10439

British Library Cataloguing in Publication Data is available.

Library of Congress Catalog Card Number: 96–10439
ISBN: 0–275–95640–7
ISSN: 0890–7161

First published in 1996

Praeger Publishers, 88 Post Road West, Westport, CT 06881
An imprint of Greenwood Publishing Group, Inc.

Printed in the United States of America

The paper used in this book complies with the
Permanent Paper Standard issued by the National
Information Standards Organization (Z39.48–1984).

10 9 8 7 6 5 4 3 2

Copyright Acknowledgment

    The author and publisher are grateful for permission to reproduce
portions of the following copyrighted material:
    From *Amusing Ourselves to Death* by Neil Postman. Copyright © 1985
by Neil Postman. Used by permission of Viking Penguin, a division of
Penguin Books USA Inc.
    Neil Postman. From *Amusing Ourselves to Death*. Viking Penguin. 1985.
Copyright © 1985 by Neil Postman. All rights reserved.

To my mother, Kitty Newman

Of all the living things on earth,
    I think there is no other:
Friends and aunts—all alike—
    But none so dear as Mother.
Who comforts you when you're in trouble?
    Who says, "Don't mind it, dear!"?
Who makes it vanish like a bubble?
    None but Mother dear.

> *—Poem composed by my mother*
> *as a young child, not long*
> *before the death of her own*
> *mother*

Contents

Acknowledgments

I thank the following institutions for facilitating my research and writing during the time in which this study was conceived and completed: The Social Sciences and Humanities Research Council of Canada, which awarded me a research grant for the period 1991–1994; and the University of Guelph, which granted me sabbatical leave of absence for the academic year 1995–1996. I gratefully acknowledge the encouragement and enlightenment that I have received for so many years now from my parents, Kate and Louis Newman; my teacher and friend, Elmer Sprague; my colleagues and friends, Michael Ruse and Brian Calvert; and colleagues in the Canadian Theological Society. I am also grateful to two dear friends, the late Stephen H. Gibson and the late Jakob Amstutz, for their help and their wisdom. And I thank Nina Pearlstein and G. Nick Street of Greenwood Publishing Group for their generous attention to the manuscript and their kindness to the author.

CHAPTER ONE

Competition Between Religion and Television: Basic Issues and Concerns

Anyone given to serious, disciplined reflection on the present and future condition of culture in Western societies will eventually come to consider at length the importance for culture of religion and of television; and while these two phenomena will be considered by that person individually, and in relation to any number of other phenomena, they are also likely to be considered, at least in passing, in relation to each other. Even those not given to disciplined reflection on culture may acknowledge, when relevant subjects arise in everyday conversation, that religion and television are both important and pervasive influences in their society, and moreover, that the formation of the judgment and character of individuals in their society, and the formation of the ethos of the society itself, depend significantly not only on religion and television individually, but also on their relations. After some reflection, even amateur cultural theorists should also be able to see that the relations between religion and television in Western societies are to a great extent, though not exclusively, competitive; and they will be able to understand that the future condition of culture in their society, and societies very much like it, depends substantially on the developmental consequences of this competition.

The subject of competition between religion and television has, if only indirectly, received considerable attention, particularly from insecure religionists disturbed by the threat posed by television programming to traditional religious beliefs, values, and attitudes, but also, especially of late, from students of mass communications theory and even from general cultural theorists. But as even the most thoughtful discussions of the subject have to this point in time been somewhat narrow, I shall endeavor in the pages that follow to consider competition between religion and television from a wider, more general, and more abstract perspective, one that could be appropriately characterized as "philosophical." Wider reflection on this or any other subject invariably leads to a kind and a degree of understanding that are not available to those who are exclusively concerned with the immediate, specific, and concrete. Being philosophical has never been in fashion, and despite recent advances in civilization, it has come to seem even stranger in contemporary life as a result of philosophy's own unsuccessful competition with television and other mass media of communication. But even though few people these days have the patience or the spiritual and intellectual wherewithal to approach a subject philosophically, those who do usually have something distinctive and valuable to contribute to their society's understanding of a subject.

I shall assume here that despite the notorious ambiguities inherent in them, the terms *religion, television,* and *competition* are basically understandable to the reader. It may be impossible to define satisfactorily the term *religion*, but working with certain paradigms, we generally associate religion with a commitment to a certain kind of worldview involving metaphysical, ethical, emotive, and other elements; this commitment ordinarily is accompanied by such things as ritual practices, association with a community of believers, a sense of the "transcendent" or "supernatural," and an antipathy toward materialism. The primary paradigm of a religion, or of religion as such, is ordinarily one's own particular religion. For most people in Western societies, the primary paradigm of a religion is Christianity. For these people, the secondary paradigms are the monotheistic religions, Judaism and Islam; the tertiary paradigms are such "major world religions" as Hinduism, Buddhism, and Shintoism; and all other religions are generally seen as representing "borderline instances" which might just as well be regarded as, say, philosophies, ideologies, or commitments to some "secular" form of worldview. *Television* in different contexts may refer to a technological process or a technological product, to an appliance or to the programming transmitted through that appliance, to an industry or a form of experience and culture, or to several of these things simultaneously. By *competition*, we understand generally the striving of two or more for the same object,[1] but here again there are nuances of interpretation regarding various issues.[2] For example, is competition in its primary sense necessarily public? Does competition necessarily involve rules? Does it require a substantial degree of awareness? And is it conceived in terms of a win-lose outcome? The ambiguities inherent in these three key terms should be kept in mind, and we must constantly strive to be as sensitive as possible to the precise significance of each term in its particular context; but we are nevertheless justified in regarding most uses of the three terms as representing "ordinary" rather than "technical" language.

Several fundamental questions are at the core of this investigation.

1. In what ways, and to what extent, can the relations between religion and television be properly regarded as competitive in the primary sense of the term?

2. In what ways are these competitive relations important for culture and civilization, and more specifically, in what ways, and to what extent, do they represent a positive force, or a negative force, with respect to cultural advancement?

3. Who represents religion and television in the competitive encounter of the two phenomena, what motivates them to enter into competition, and for what particular objects are they striving?

4. How does competition between religion and television relate to non-competitive forms of interaction between the two phenomena?

5. What is the precise relationship between religion and television as forms of experience and culture, and has television to some extent taken over the role in Western societies previously played by religion?

6. When is competition between religion and television fair competition and when is it unfair, and is most competition between the two fair or unfair?

7. What degree of awareness do the representatives of religion and television bring to their competitive encounters?

8. What can be done to improve the quality of competition between religion and television and to minimize that competition between them which has a negative influence upon culture and civilization?

Although these questions are for the most part more abstract than the questions about competition between religion and television that are normally addressed by religious critics of the mass media, broadcasting industry executives, producers, bureaucrats, and social–scientific communications theorists, consideration of these questions should help such people, and help us, to provide more profound answers to the concrete questions. As it happens, to answer satisfactorily the abstract questions, we sometimes have to consider the concrete ones, for one cannot philosophize in a vacuum. Accordingly, along the way, we shall find ourselves considering here some of the specific controversies concerning religion and television that have arisen in recent years in the public forum. For example, is television programming in a country like the United States, Canada, or the United Kingdom dominated and manipulated by political liberals and secular humanists, or is it perhaps dominated rather by materialists from the world of big business? Do news programs on commercial television networks offer adequate coverage of religious matters? Is the "electronic church" too strong a presence on television? Do certain types of television programming promote materialism and make people stupid?

Such concrete questions, which have already been much explored in the public forum, are not the principal concern of this study, so one will be disappointed if one is expecting here the kind of "practical" observations and recommendations that one routinely finds in the writings of professional and amateur "media critics." As this inquiry is a humanistic rather than a social-scientific inquiry, one will not find very much here in the way of "data." This study will be of use primarily to a reader who believes that the abstract questions are worth asking. Over the centuries philosophers and other humanists have provided us with insights into how to go about answering these questions constructively.

Humanists continue to discourse at great length about religion and religious subjects, but they have had relatively little to say about television. In 1977, religion professor Robert S. Alley took note of academic humanists' professional neglect of the phenomenon:

[C]ritical comments from the academic community have often decried the deleterious effects of television viewing upon the cultures. Rightfully concerned over quality and the preservation of cultural strength, professors have found little time for constructive criticism.... [A]cademics are often loathe to accept television research as scholarly unless it is done within the confines of the departments of psychology and sociology. It seems to be off limits for those who practice seriously the disciplines of literature, history, philosophy, and ethics.[3]

Not much has changed since Alley made this observation, and if the little that academic humanists do say about television is not taken as seriously as it ought to be, the fault lies partly with the humanistic community itself, which has not demonstrated that it is prepared to take the subject as seriously as media critics, bureaucrats, and social-scientific communications theorists take it. Still, even the most earnest and diligent humanistic students of the mass media, whose work is deemed eminently respectable by their fellow humanistic scholars, cannot reasonably expect the common sort of media critic, broadcast industry executive, or bureaucrat—much less the general public, with its countless interests and concerns—to welcome their intellectual contributions with tremendous enthusiasm.

The most general aim of this study is simply to draw on methods and insights from the philosophy of culture, the philosophy of religion, and the rapidly developing field of the philosophy of mass communications to "illuminate" or "shed light on" a cultural phenomenon of far-reaching importance. It is my hope that by taking a "wider" perspective in considering competition between religion and television, we will be able to see beyond debates that have thus far generated more heat than light.

But I would already be leaving you in the dark if I did not provide you at the outset with a more focused indication of what I am trying to accomplish, and indeed, what I am trying to establish. There is no hidden agenda in this study, and I shall try to lay all my cards on the table here so that you have a clear enough idea of where I am coming from and where I am trying to go.

First, it seems to me that if we are satisfactorily to understand the general cultural relations, competitive or otherwise, between religion and television, we must give close attention to both phenomena; we must be prepared not only to understand both, but to assess the cultural value of both, and to see the similarities as well as the differences between them in their relation to their cultural context. So, although this book is about television, it is just as much about religion and about culture; it is not just an exploration of television programming from a religious perspective, but an exploration of religion, television, and their cultural relations from a philosophical perspective. Later in Chapter 1, and throughout the study, we shall be concentrating our attention on institutionalized religion; and if you are puzzled by all the attention given to religion itself, it is probably because you have not been able to shake off the assumption that this study is primarily about television. In this inquiry, I am as interested in religion as television, and as interested in culture as religion, but I am very much interested in all three things, which are extremely important in my own life as well as the lives of countless other people.

I hope to establish, or at least confirm and strengthen your opinion, that competition between religion and television is a complex, multifaceted phenomenon that has been oversimplified in the analyses of polemicists and ideologists of various stripes, and that properly understanding it, particularly in terms of the competition between forms of experience and culture, enables one to make sounder and more informed judgments not only about certain major issues of social and cultural policy but about the role that religion and television play and ought to play in one's own life and in the lives of those whom one is in a position to influence.

Much of what will be said in these pages can be fairly construed as a defense of television and "television people" from certain kinds of criticism. But it is not a basic aim of this study to defend television and "television people," and it is certainly not an aim of this study to show religion and religionists in a bad light. There is much about television and television programming that troubles me, and I believe that even at its best television is not as important for civilization and human progress as is sound, constructive religious commitment. However, for reasons that I shall be indicating later on, "television people" generally cannot explain, assess, and openly pass judgment on religious phenomena in the way or to the extent that so many religionists can confidently speak

in private and in public on the strengths and shortcomings of television
and television programming. Thus, the task has fallen to me to say certain things about religion and its relation to television and to culture that
few if any television executives, producers, artists, and technicians are
in a position to say.

Finally, I should say from the outset that this study represents in part
an extension of a long-term project to contribute to the understanding of
how religious bigotry is to be confronted and minimized. Undoubtedly,
my special interest in the problem of religious bigotry has influenced
much of what is said in the pages that follow about religion and religionists; but I do not see how any thoughtful person can consider religion
in a cultural context without paying some serious attention to how religious bigotry not only subverts civilization generally but subverts the
positive cultural influence of authentic religion. And surely religious critics of television—or of anything else—have a certain obligation to try to
make clear in their own minds how it has been possible for the most
spiritual impulses of human beings to be distorted in such a way that
they have given rise to the worst forms of barbarism. Being mindful of
the importance of the evils of religious intolerance, prejudice, and hatred
is, in any case, consistent with the conviction that authentic religion is
at the core of a civilized and civilizing culture.

The expression, "competition between religion and television," may
have a strange ring, but the phenomenon that it designates has been
usefully characterized by various students of the relations between religion and the mass media. As we consider representative characterizations of the phenomenon, we should note important differences in tone
and interpretation.

Consider first the phenomenon as characterized by certain Christian
critics of television. (Bear in mind that these critics favor a certain kind
of religion and also that they are not necessarily critical of all aspects of
television or television programming.) William F. Fore argues that,

[T]oday television is beginning to usurp a role which until recently has been the
role of the church in our society, namely, to shape our system of values, embody
our faith, and express our cultural essence. This shift, from a religious center to
what I call a technological center, is ominous. . . . The shift is not yet irreversible,
but it soon will be if viewers do not begin to recognize the problem and learn
how to cope with television in ways which allow them to accept its benefits
without succumbing to its worldview.[4]

"Television today, whether the viewers know it or not, and whether the
television industry itself knows it or not, is competing not merely for
our attention and dollars, but for our very souls."[5] Focusing on televi-

sion, William Kuhns writes, "in effect, the entertainment media may not only be usurping functions which once belonged to religion, but likewise restructuring the very shape of belief."[6] He then asks, "What then *is* the church to become? One suggestion: a vital source in society for creating a critical awareness of the entertainment milieu, a kind of anti-environment."[7] Donald Porter holds that

The success or failure of a TV programme or series is measured by the number of viewers it had. So the entertainment is usually tailored to suit what the majority of people want. Thus TV normally reflects the tastes, standards and interests of the majority. . . . [B]ecause it caters for a majority interest, and the majority of people aren't Christians, there will be some things also that will be unhelpful to us [Christians] and sometimes even harmful.[8]

And Donald E. Wildmon insists that, "the organized church in America faces the greatest threat to its existence since our country was founded," as "there is an intentional effort among many of the leaders of our media to reshape our society, to replace the Christian view of man as our foundation with the humanist view of man."[9]

These four characterizations of competition between religion and television have important features in common. Each has been put forward by someone who regards himself as a representative and defender of the Christian faith, and each portrays television, or some dominant force in the television industry, as a major threat to Christianity. Only the first of the four characterizations refers directly to competition as such, but the implicit reference to competition in the others is not hard to detect. However, nuances of emphasis are worth noting. One characterization contrasts the religious with the technological; another focuses on the chasm between religion and entertainment; a third emphasizes the conflict between a non-Christian majority and a Christian minority; and the last sees a cabal of secular humanists conspiring against the values and attitudes of a Christian majority. In fact, the four writers quoted are not consistent in focusing on the theme with which they are associated above. But what is noteworthy at this point is that whether they explicitly identify it or not, these Christian critics of television, television programming, and television executives all see their principal paradigm of religion, which they associate with the soundest possible foundations for their society's culture, as threatened by, and involved in a competitive struggle with, a cultural or anticultural agenda that they associate with television. And while these critics all recognize that television can be, and sometimes has been, put to the service of promoting Christian ideas, values, and attitudes, they regard the threat posed by television as primary.

Prudence usually dictates that defenders of television, television programming, and the television industry not attack Christianity or religion as such for being a threat to the institution or phenomenon that they are defending. For many reasons, not the least being that religion is an ancient form of experience and culture while television is something relatively very new, it would sound foolish if a defender of television were to use the kind of language used in the four characterizations cited above. But some defenders of television and television programming do routinely criticize those that they portray as religious fanatics, reactionaries, or conservatives for maleficently interfering with television as an art and an industry. In their defense of the forms of freedom of expression with which they associate television at its most constructive, there is often the implicit thesis that what television programming provides society is, on balance, better than what most religious critics of television have to offer.

Consider, for example, these remarks by Steven Starker:

The original "crusades" were military expeditions undertaken by the Christian nations in the eleventh to thirteenth centuries to win the Holy Land from Islam. The same term, however, may be applied to any remedial enterprise undertaken in the name of moral or religious outrage; its application to the cycles of attack upon the mass media therefore seems quite appropriate. Crusades, of course, always have political aspects. Moral issues serve as rallying points, and they are readily seized upon by those in search of a political following.[10]

Although essentially descriptive on the surface, this passage, which explains the title of a book that encourages readers to help those who represent television and other mass media to hold their ground against moralists and religionists who would undermine their autonomy and influence, reminds readers of the dark side of religion, and specifically, of its association with bigotry, superstition, violence, deviousness, hypocrisy, and all those dimensions of barbarism that to many reflective students of history are symbolized by the medieval Crusades.

Although defenders of television in the Western democracies rarely attack religion as such, or even Christianity, they regularly contrast the positive influence of much television programming with the maleficent aspects of the agenda of the "religious right." The bolder among them allude to the competition between the forces of freedom and democracy represented by the liberal mass media and the forces of authoritarianism and privilege represented by entrenched ecclesiastical institutions. There are also critics of the television industry who have suggested that its executives and programmers have been insufficiently competitive in their dealings with religious conservatives, or at the very least have exhibited cowardice in denying a proper forum to critics of institutionalized religion. The noted secular humanist, Paul Kurtz, has observed that "secular humanism is highly skeptical of the supernatural view of reality, belief in the afterlife, and other Biblical claims, but there are almost no careful critiques of religious faith on commercial television. Instead the televangelists pour forth *pro*biblical propaganda that is virtually unchallenged."[11]

Even when religion is not specifically mentioned, it is often implicitly indicated when liberal and leftist ideologists defend television from attacks on it by their conservative and rightist counterparts, or when they criticize television for being insufficiently critical of entrenched elites. Thus, it is not necessary for someone like Herbert I. Schiller to make specific reference to the "religious right" when he remarks that

Organizations, groups, and individuals who constituted the fringe right in the immediate postwar years have moved into the center of respectability. They now dominate the columns and airtime of the mainstream media. It is not that conservative thought and expression were absent from establishment opinion-making in earlier years. Rather, it is the near preemption of informational and cultural space by that perspective in the 1980s.[12]

Schiller expects his readers to be aware of the agenda shared by capitalists and powerful, self-serving religious leaders long before he reminds them, by way of example, of the "trials and antics of Jimmy Swaggart, whose television ministry took in over $120 million a year."[13] Although they rarely make the point explicitly, most liberal and leftist critics of television would like to see the development of television programming that directly confronts the corruption of religious elites and particularly those religious elites allied with political and business elites.

Some humanists have attempted to provide a purely descriptive characterization of competition between religion and television. Regardless of whether they are themselves committed to a religious worldview, they have endeavored to offer a fundamentally nonjudgmental analysis of what they take to be an important feature of contemporary culture. So, for example, Gregor T. Goethals, despite theological interests, has no ax to grind when analytically observing that television has come to provide a substitute for sacraments,[14] and that,

Today, communities such as churches continue to provide their members with myths and visual symbols. At the same time, however, commercial television, especially as it has developed over the last twenty years [1961–1981], has played a major role in expressing and shaping our values. It has done so by weaving a web of easily understood and accessible images that provides fragmented groups with public symbols.[15]

Quite a few cultural theorists who are not specifically concerned with propping up religion in contemporary life have been moved to note that

television as a form of technology or medium of communication, regardless of its program content, is necessarily brought into competition
with traditional religion. For one thing, television, along with other contemporary forces that shape mass culture, by its very nature can effectively perform tasks that once could be performed only through religion,
and it can do so without the imposing demands that genuine religious
commitment makes. For example, as John Phelan has noted:

In the end, what has done the most damage to organized churches, particularly
the Roman Catholic, is not so much the intellectual questioning and doubt of
enlightenment or existentialist provenance, which have so little interest for the
average secondary tribesman in any event. It is the substitution of secular mass
culture for previous popular Christianity, with its penchant for the quasi-magical
or "mechanical," a tendency so well served today by the putatively godless.[16]

Again, with its remarkable ability to tell stories, it almost effortlessly
performs a role that was once performed primarily by religious narrative, and in the eyes of some, such as Quentin J. Schultze, in this respect,
"[T]elevision *functions* as the Bible for millions of people."[17] In having
become the new "cultural storyteller,"[18] it is "an agent of norms and
values as much as of news and information," and it "fulfills this function
very much in the way traditional storytellers did."[19]

Television also competes with traditional religion by transforming it
in ways that are unacceptable to many religious leaders. The main point
to note here is not that many religious leaders are inclined to be theologically conservative or self-serving, although many indeed are, nor is
it simply that television programmers generally handle religious subjects
carelessly and superficially, although again many of them indeed often
do. Even the role consciously and unconsciously played by liberal religionists and atheists in the transformation is ultimately of secondary importance, although we shall have to consider it later on. What is most
striking to leading scholars in the field is the extent to which the nature
of television as a form of technology or a medium of communication
forces television to handle religious subject matter narrowly and at times
one-dimensionally. In Neil Postman's view, a basic problem here is that,
"[N]ot everything is *televisible*. Or to put it more precisely, what is televised is transformed from what it was to something else, which may or
may not preserve its former essence."[20] In Postman's view, entertainment
is the "supra-ideology of all discourse on television. No matter what is
depicted or from what point of view, the overarching presumption is
that it is there for our amusement and pleasure."[21] He adds, "[T]he television screen itself has a strong bias toward a psychology of secularism,"[22] and television is "a form of graven imagery far more alluring
than a golden calf."[23] Interestingly, Postman feels that television is most

useful when presenting "junk-entertainment," for when it co-opts serious modes of discourse, it turns them into "entertainment packages."[24]

Peter G. Horsfield, who has made a careful study of religious television in the United States, approaches this problem from another perspective. Acutely aware of how many in the church have historically attempted to adapt new forms of mass communication to the church's purposes,[25] he observes that others in the church have worried about the dangers involved in this program:

There has been a persistent body of people who question the use of mass media in religious communication as an inherent contradiction in terms. The essence of Christian communication according to many is its responsiveness, its service to human need, and its affirmation of the individual. To speak of "mass" communication is an impossibility.... Such one-way communication of a religious message eventually strips the message of its interactive, existential dimensions.[26]

If this is the case, then religious television, or the use of television by religious communicators, accords with rather than deviates from the fundamental competitiveness between religion and television. Quentin Schultze makes the related point that television as a form of technology and medium of communication can at best do justice only to certain types of theology:

[T]elevision favors experientially validated theologies over systematically argued ones. Pentecostals, neo-Pentecostals, and charismatics find the tube an attractive and effective medium, whereas reformational Protestants do not quite know what to do with it. Lengthy sermons, delivered in a literary fashion and based on systematic theology, generally flop on the tube.[27]

Moreover, Schultze argues that, "personal prayer, meditation, and reflection are difficult for all of us in the television age. We're losing grasp of the importance of silence and solitude in our relationships with God and each other."[28] Stewart M. Hoover explicitly acknowledges the competitive aspect of the relations between traditional religion and television that is ironically reflected in the success of the "electronic church." He says, "[D]enominational television simply cannot compete with the electronic church in sophistication, reach, and visibility. Denominations have found themselves in a battle for national prominence and attention that is loaded against them."[29]

In the eyes of Stephen R. Lawhead, such polite and dignified characterizations of competition between religion and television miss the key point. "A Christian's view of pop culture is directly determined by what he or she believes about the devil."[30] Indeed,

The devil's work on TV, it seems to me, is basically a work of deception, of masking reality in such a way as to give it a slightly different face. . . . Christians affirm the fact that natural man is lost. Television describes in a multitude of ways the ascendancy of natural man—free, honest, hard-working, and just, having no need of faith, salvation, or reconciliation with his Maker. Religion is a crutch for the weak-hearted, the feeble-minded. This is the gospel of TV-land.[31]

Most of the theorists and critics who directly or indirectly address issues related to competition between religion and television are very much impressed by what they take to be the extremely powerful cultural or anticultural impact of television and television programming. Certain common themes run through their various characterizations of the power and influence of television and television programming, but again differences in tone and interpretation should be noted.

Common sense suggests to most of us that television has a powerful influence on our society through its influence on the beliefs, values, and attitudes of so many of the individuals who make up our society. It is, after all, one of the "mass" media of communication. Many if not most of us spend more time watching television than we spend on all but a small number of other activities. Most of us can think of a significant number of people we know that we would regard as addicted to television watching. In casual conversation with people at work, school, and the market, we may well find ourselves discussing television more than any other subject besides the weather. And it is no secret that many advertisers spend enormous sums of money on television commercials because experience and research have shown them that such expenditures normally yield handsome returns. Moreover, the characterizations of competition between religion and television that were cited above provide us with a wide range of ideas about the cultural or anticultural impact of television, television programming, and television executives. They refer, for example, to how television caters to the majority interest, successfully aims at entertainment, weaves a web of accessible images, responds to the viewers' need for the quasi-magical, and effectively serves as a cultural storyteller.

While there have been many detailed psychological studies of the effects of television viewing, for our purposes here it is not necessary to go far beyond common sense in order to understand television's special power in relation to traditional forms of religious influence. Thus, as Hoover points out, television derives much of its power from

Its presence in the everyday lives and consciousness of its viewers. It is not like education, or government, or even the church—sociocultural institutions whose presence is felt in individual lives only episodically. Instead, it is there, in the home or the workplace. If survey data are to be believed, it is one of the most satisfying and attractive activities of contemporary life.[32]

David Porter observes along these lines that, "You don't have to make any effort except for switching it on. . . . It's there in your house, and it will perform for you whenever you want it to."[33] Schultze, who believes that, "roughly speaking, the American lifestyle can be divided into three major activities: sleeping, working, and watching television,"[34] is also impressed by the "free" and "effortless" aspects of television watching,[35] although as we noted above, he is even more impressed by television's ability to perform certain roles traditionally performed by and through religion.

Especially since the publication and widespread discussion of the major works of Marshall McLuhan, most students of mass communications have been careful not to overemphasize the influence of the content of a medium like television at the expense of the influence of the new and unique form of perception that the medium demands:

Our conventional response to all media, namely that it is how they are used that counts, is the numb stance of the technological idiot. For the "content" of a medium is like the juicy piece of meat carried by the burglar to distract the watchdog of the mind. The effect of the medium is made strong and intense just because it is given another medium as "content."[36]

For McLuhan, television must be understood as a "cool" medium, one of "low definition," as "little is given and much has to be filled in" by the viewer-listener.[37] It influences us more through the changes demanded by a new technology than through its "content": "Physiologically, man in the normal use of technology (or his variously extended body) is perpetually modified by it and in turn finds ever new ways of modifying his technology."[38] Those who operate mass media like television for the owners demonstrate a "peculiar bias" in their concern about program content, but the owners of the media, concerned with media as power, know that this power has much less to do with "content" than with the nature of the medium itself.[39] "All media are active metaphors in their power to translate experience into new forms."[40]

McLuhan's extreme ideas were articulated by an enthusiast who to some extent allowed his judgment to be clouded by his imaginative insights, so that we can perhaps appreciate the dissatisfaction of a critic like Gunnar Andrén, who, moving to another extreme, writes that

Marshall McLuhan's notorious formula "the medium is the message" is patently absurd. First, it is certainly always possible to make an analytical distinction between the medium and that which is mediated through it, i.e., its contents or the messages expressed by means of it. Secondly, what affects the audience cannot be the medium *per se*, but the contents presented in a certain medium, the concrete manifestations of certain ideas or images.[41]

But McLuhan's ideas have had a salutary impact on mass communications theory in drawing attention to the fact that the power of a medium like television does not reside exclusively or perhaps even primarily in those contents. "TV has changed our sense-lives and our mental processes"[42] with its "mosaic image"[43]; it "involves us in moving depth,"[44] and, "Not even the most lucid understanding of the peculiar force of [such] a medium can head off the ordinary 'closure' of the senses that causes us to conform to the pattern of experience presented."[45]

Much influenced by McLuhan,[46] Neil Postman suggests that, "As the influence of print wanes, the content of politics, religion, education, and anything else that comprises public business must change and be recast in terms that are most suitable to television;"[47] for, "[A]lthough culture is a creation, speech, it is recreated anew by every medium of communication—from painting to hieroglyphs to the alphabet to television. Each medium, like language itself, makes possible a unique mode of discourse by providing a new orientation for thought, for expression, for sensibility."[48] Television has become "our culture's principal mode of knowing about itself. Therefore—and this is the critical point—how television stages the world becomes the model for how the world is properly to be staged."[49]

But Postman is very much the enthusiast as well, and it is useful to contrast his views with those of certain astute observers who believe that the cultural or anticultural impact of television is too easily exaggerated. Consider first these general observations by Martin H. Seiden:

The "power of the media" is a cliché to which reference is almost always made in discussion of this sort. This power has been accepted as real, yet it consists principally of the ability to reach a phenomenal number of people at the same time. If by power one also means the ability to influence, it still remains to be proven that man's ability to direct others has increased because of technology. The existence since the dawn of history of mass movements and totalitarian regimes indicates that political and social ills would still exist, with or without mass communications. One should not forget that Moses, Confucius, Buddha, Jesus, Mohammed, and Marx did not have the benefit of today's sophisticated technology and advertising budgets, yet their points of view and their personalities still command a great deal more attention than that of any of our contemporaries. Perhaps we have forgotten that the key to influencing people is, after all, ideas rather than technology.[50]

Although even the most profound ideas have always needed to be promoted—and have generally required more in the way of sophisticated promotion than simple ideas—Seiden's main points are worth taking, and in his helpful reference to great religious leaders, he reminds us of an important dimension of competition between religion and television.

Social psychologist Dennis Howitt, having undertaken extensive research into the influence of the media, is convinced of "the great difficulty of using the mass media to manipulate the attitudes and opinions of members of the audience,"[51] and he suggests that, "[M]ost of the more vocal claims about the good and bad effects of the mass media are mere assertions based on opinion rather than scientific evidence."[52] With respect to religion and television in particular, Peter G. Horsfield has concluded from research that, "There are very few people who may experience some form of religious conversion by television alone who continue in that change through extended involvement within an interactive Christian group,"[53] and Schultze has made the equally important observation that,

Christians on average view the same amount of television as non-Christians; moreover, they tend to watch the same programmes, except that believers tend to watch more religious broadcasts. Evangelicals may have distinctive views of Scripture and of the need for personal conversion, but they are as likely to watch a given soap opera or situation comedy as are people for whom Christ is merely a myth. Apparently, evangelicals' relationships to Christ have little or no impact on their television viewing.[54]

We must also not underestimate the extent to which television and television programming reflect rather than determine the shape of the culture of the particular society in which they function. Even when television programming does not, in Porter's words, "cater for a majority interest," it "normally reflects the tastes, standards and interests of the majority."[55] And more generally, despite the view of certain media critics that most television programming is controlled by a cabal of Machiavellian conspirators, television programming is substantially determined by prevailing cultural beliefs, values, and attitudes, so that, for example, as Schultze has observed, "Television's sins . . . are also the sins of American culture,"[56] and as Starker has suggested, there are ordinarily striking similarities between critiques of the mass media and critiques of mass culture.[57]

A related point worth considering is that even some of the most severe critics of television and television programming continue to watch television. Schultze has remarked that, "We all joke about how bad television is, but we still watch it."[58] This, of course, is an overstatement in several ways. Not all people are convinced that television and television programming are fundamentally "bad," and those who are are not necessarily given to joking about the matter; and, of course, there are people who do not watch television, and some of these fear being corrupted by it. Still, sociologist Steve Bruce has helpfully commented that,

The power of television is a curious phenomenon. Most people are convinced that the medium is extremely powerful and many worry that showing violence, for example, on the small screen will cause people to be more violent. But when asked if watching violence on television makes them more violent, such people always deny that it has an effect on *them*. It is always someone else who is supposedly moved in this manner. We seem torn between our own self-knowledge that television has little effect and the plausible suggestion that anything which people watch that much must be doing something.[59]

There is some overstatement here too, for some people are convinced that television viewing has a negative influence on their own behavior as well as the behavior of others. It is almost certainly true, however, that people who engage in mass media criticism ordinarily believe that they are substantially less vulnerable to the negative impact of mass media than most people are; and while they may generally be right, concrete and specific judgments in this area will often be highly subjective and sometimes rather arbitrary. "Surveying the voluminous body of literature attacking the media," Starker notes, "it may seem surprising that America and its inhabitants have survived at all."[60]

We have seen how when they consider the matter of competition between religion and television, religious intellectuals and others who believe strongly in the importance of religion for contemporary cultural life may find it appropriate to portray television and those responsible for television programming as "usurpers." To make their case satisfactorily, they must establish three things. They must first establish that in performing certain roles over the centuries, religion, or a particular form of religion, has, on balance, substantially contributed to the advancement of culture and civilization. They must also establish that television, whether those responsible for television programming are aware of it or not, has come to take over, or at least threatens to take over, some or all of religion's most important traditional functions. And finally they must establish that television is not capable of performing those functions as well as religion historically did and still can.

One can, of course, offer a characterization of competition between religion and television that does not cast television, television programming, and those responsible for television programming in the role of "usurpers." One can say, for example, that television has simply replaced or superseded religion in performing certain social and cultural functions, and that it has done so because it can by certain criteria do a "better" job than religion in that regard. Or one can say that only time will tell whether television performs those functions worse (or better) than religion traditionally has. One can also say that the main things for which religion and television compete, such as, say, attention, are such that it is inappropriate to think in terms of one's usurping the other's role. (In competing for something like attention, religion has to compete not only with television but with such things as professional vocation, liberal education, leisure activities, and aesthetic pursuits, none of which would be characterized by anyone other than a religious fanatic as involving a usurpation of a religious prerogative.)

But if one is to establish that television is involved in a genuine usurpation of some important role traditionally and properly performed by religion, then one has three separate tasks to fulfill. The first, as we have noted, is to show that throughout the centuries, religion has contributed significantly to the advancement of civilization and the general melioration of the quality of human existence by performing certain functions. Many religious critics of television do not defend or even explicitly advance such a position. They are usually "preaching to the converted"; and when they are, they realize that the positive cultural value of religion or of a particular religion is taken for granted by almost all of their readers or listeners, and that not much is to be gained by beginning their critique of television with a careful, detailed apologetic. Indeed, they may well be prudent in avoiding such an apologetic, for what they value most in religious experience and culture may be quite different from what certain readers or listeners value most. Furthermore, to speak at length of religion in terms of its cultural functions is to risk appearing to be more of the functionalist, pragmatist, or utilitarian than one wants the audience to recognize. (In any case, even the most fuzzy-minded religious liberals try to believe that their faith has some basic connection with truth and reality and is not simply something that enables certain personality types to get on with the business of living in a happier and more socially constructive way.) Still, if the religious media critic's pronouncement that television is usurping a traditional role of religion is to be more than a rhetorical device or an appeal to dogma, then she must provide her audience with some insight into what that role is and why the performance of it is conducive to cultural advancement. And of course, doing so is even more important when she is not merely preaching to the converted but is engaged in communication with reflective, open-minded inquirers seeking a deeper understanding of contemporary or philosophical cultural issues. More often than not, the religious media critic's conception of the cultural value of religion is only to be inferred from her critical comments on the shortcomings of television and television programming.

When the religious media critic (that is, the religionist criticizing the media rather than the critic of the religious media) specifically identifies the traditional cultural functions of religion, she risks being either vague and platitudinous or arbitrary and incorrect. Think back to William Fore's comment that, "[T]oday television is beginning to usurp a role which until recently has been the role of the church in our society, namely, to shape our system of values, embody our faith, and express our cultural essence."[61] Even if one has some idea of what Fore has in mind here, one can hardly be certain, for Fore's language is not very precise. And many will take exception to Fore's unqualified assertion that it has been the role of the church alone to shape our system of values, for systems of values have historically been shaped by all sorts of things, from genetic inheritance, parental upbringing, and the arbitrary will of self-serving despots to reason, philosophy, and the fine arts. When Fore later goes on to sermonize dogmatically about "the fall," the sin of pride, and the chief end of life being to glorify God rather than to be happy,[62] one may well be struck by how different Fore's faith and system of values are from those of one's own spiritual tradition.

If one moves from dogmatic theology to philosophy of religion, one is able to take a broader view of this matter of the cultural functions of religion. Over the centuries, religion has performed an extraordinarily wide variety of roles, and even most contemporary religionists will be prepared to acknowledge that it is a good thing, on the whole, that some of its traditional roles have been taken over by secular disciplines and institutions. In advanced societies like our own, where the church is in a sense "separated" from the state, the church no longer performs a role that it performed in theocratic societies, but that is almost always a good thing. The church no longer forces scientists like Galileo to affirm that the sun revolves around the earth. Having given up its role as authority on natural-scientific matters has not, on balance, harmed the church or society. Again, whatever their failings, pluralistic societies, in which the church has surrendered its traditional role of imposing a socially unifying worldview on recalcitrant yet high-minded minorities, are in important ways far more civilized than those that they have superseded. And of course we must not forget that in performing certain traditional roles, religious institutions have been responsible for all sorts of evils, including bigotry, violence, superstition, and oppression.

Even religious media critics who are highly critical of television programming grant that television has done a considerable amount of good. If pressed, these critics would probably admit that substantial benefits have followed from religion's having had to share its influence with television. Television programs inform and provide general knowledge;[63] they capture important myths and heroes of our age;[64] they provide relaxation and escape, psychological compensation, security and stability, guidance on how to cope, a sense of belonging, and a rich fantasy world;[65] they teach sound moral lessons;[66] they evoke moral criticism and help people to recognize the moral inadequacies of the modern world;[67] and sometimes they even promote idealistic and effective political activism.[68] In all of these ways, television performs roles or functions that in past centuries were performed largely by and through religion. Such sharing of some of religion's most important cultural roles cannot be dismissed as a mere "usurpation." Moreover, television programs have in various ways promoted religious beliefs, values, and attitudes; and through their competition and criticism, they have provided religious leaders, denominations, and institutions with powerful incentives to self-improvement.

Religious media critics are inclined to observe, however, that it is often precisely in the areas where television has done some good that television has done some of its greatest harm. Moreover, it is often in characterizing the failings of television that religious critics of television indicate what they take to be the important cultural functions traditionally performed by religion. Thus, they will point out that those responsible for television programming typically do the job poorly, passing on trivial information, promoting irresponsible escapism and the stability engendered by passivity, sending confusing and misleading moral messages, and creating a sense of despair in viewers overexposed to violence, ugliness, and corruption. And while these critics may acknowledge that religious leaders and institutions have themselves not always performed these functions properly, they ordinarily go on to explain certain features of television or television programming that in their view render it an ineffective and often dangerous substitute for religion.

Let us consider some of television's specific failings with respect to these functions. Television provides a great deal of useful information, but it provides even more in the way of trivial information. Perhaps that is why the phrase "educational television" usually brings to mind only a handful of stations, series, and specials, and most nondramatic programming is assumed to be only secondarily educational at most. Our society's most distinguished thinkers and researchers receive little opportunity to make their ideas and data known to television audiences, but entertainers have almost unlimited opportunity to make known their opinions and to inform audiences about their latest performance, and how their latest marriage is faring. Even news programs on the commercial networks provide little in the way of important information, and people forget most broadcast news stories almost immediately after hearing them. McLuhan keenly observed that among reflective people, in the near future, "Education will become recognized as civil defense against media fallout."[69] But the religious educator, who in past centuries was one of the ordinary individual's most valuable guides and "resource persons," finds it harder and harder to get people to listen.

Religion traditionally offered the lowly, the disadvantaged, and the suffering a precious escape from the misery and the drudgery of their everyday lives. If it could be an "opiate" that discouraged salutary political activism, it could also provide unique forms of hope, compassion, and peace of mind, and access to a highly spiritual form of experience, the experience of the holy, the sacred. Television also often functions as an "opiate," but the escapism associated with it rarely has anything to do with human spirituality. "People may pray for daily bread, but for many millions in advanced industrial states and, increasingly, throughout the world, cultural sustenance is delivered by the mass media of communication in a form more like burnt toast."[70] The forms of happiness and fulfillment that religious experience and participation in religious life can offer are of a wholly different order than the forms to be attained by seeing one's baseball team win or one's favorite soap opera character vindicated.

Questions about the role of television as moral educator and miseducator have generated a great deal of heat and little light, and Robert S. Alley is justifiably critical of many of his fellow religionists when he observes, "Whenever the question of ethics and TV arise [sic], religious groups generally bestir themselves as advocates of corrective action. This usually amounts to negative diatribes against personal 'immorality' of the commercial networks for 'polluting the airwaves.' The chief fault with these often repeated criticisms appears to be the assumption that a particular moral perspective is 'the' moral perspective."[71] Alley himself is prepared to regard the well-known producer of American "situation comedies," Norman Lear, as a genuine "American moralist,"[72] although Lear has been a principal target of criticism by reactionary religious media critics like Donald Wildmon.[73] Still, if the moral lessons and messages communicated by religious teachers have often been confused and misleading, they at least provide some direct connection to a great repository of moral wisdom; but television, with its preoccupation with the worldly, contemporary, profane, and pleasant, is not firmly anchored in traditional spiritual wisdom, and so it is easier for television than religion to hold up such "ideals" as power, success, wealth, and fame, and to subordinate such traditional virtues as integrity, compassion, patience, and discipline. Even when television offers religious programming, it may be largely cut off from traditional moral wisdom. Postman suggests that, "[W]hat is preached on television is not anything like the Sermon on the Mount. Religious programs are filled with good cheer. They celebrate affluence. Their featured players become celebrities. Though their messages are trivial, the shows have high ratings, or rather, *because* their messages are trivial, the shows have high ratings."[74]

Those who are concerned with the inadequacy of television as a substitute for religion rarely entertain that if those responsible for television programming worked more thoughtfully and more honestly, television could eventually be an adequate substitute for religion. Such people almost always believe that religion is not only a distinctive form of experience but is irreplaceable as a foundation for civilization and cultural progress. As part of their competitive strategy as defenders of religion, they regularly point to outstanding examples of poor television programming, and at times they sincerely plead for better programming. But we must not be misled by this behavior; in their view, no matter how good television programming is by other criteria, it is incapable of satisfactorily performing the traditional cultural functions of religion, and to the extent that it usurps religion's role, television is a threat to cultural progress, no matter how earnest, wise, and high-minded those responsible for it are. In any case, what lies at the core of their argument is not how specific television programs and programmers have bungled the tasks of informing, promoting stability, providing moral education, and so on, but rather how certain features of television programming necessarily render it ineffective and an often dangerous substitute for religion.

One such feature commonly referred to is the "passivity" promoted by television viewing. Thus, Porter writes: "All the disadvantages of television, all the bad changes it has made in our way of life, start from the place it occupies in the home. It is, first and foremost, a *passive medium*. In other words, it doesn't demand any active response from you at all."[75] Especially noteworthy is the fact that television becomes "passively antisocial": "[F]amilies forget how to talk to each other, the home stops being a place where visitors feel welcome, and the whole family structure is threatened by this polished little box."[76] The main source of the problem here is probably not the incompetence or manipulativeness of those responsible for television programming, though each of these does contribute in its own way to the problem, but rather the nature of television as a form of "mass communication," which by definition, as Michael R. Real observes, "is communication that emanates from a single individual or organizational source through electronic or mechanical coding and multiplication of the message to a relatively large, heterogeneous, and anonymous audience with only limited and indirect means of feedback."[77]

This becomes clear when we consider television's handling of religion itself. As Real states:

Mass media effectively transmit certain aspects of religion as traditionally practiced but tend to vitiate other aspects. The *unidirectional* organization of mass media systems built up for marketing purposes severely limits opportunities for the audiences to provide direct feedback to the producers of media and messages. As a result, mass media contribute to a passive, internalized religion. Believers are removed from the interactive religious exchange possible in primary face-to-face interpersonal communication.[78]

Real, however, is not concerned here with the defense of religion as such, and has broader cultural concerns than the typical religious media critic.[79]

Schultze believes that, "Popular television programming encourages us to become passive audiences awaiting the latest commercial messages and political propaganda. Few programs really foster thoughtful viewing."[80] And again, "Television probably interrupts opportunities for genuine family discussion more than it fosters them. It tends to make our thoughts and feelings for each other even more private."[81] Here Schultze does to some extent associate the passivity produced in television viewers with the manipulativeness of those responsible for "popular" television programming, but he is clearly aware of the problems posed by television as a medium and form of technology.

It should be clear, in any case, that religious critics of television, and some secular critics as well, see television as promoting "passivity" in several different ways. First, television does not demand active response. Again, it does not offer the same opportunities for active response that other "activities" do. Of particular importance in this regard is its discouragement of intellectual activity, for although some television programs are thought-provoking, television viewing can turn off the reflective mind in a way that reading even a silly book or participating in an unimportant social exchange cannot. Moreover, while television viewing can stimulate all sorts of social activity, as for example in providing one with subjects for discussion or in being an impetus to social activism, it easily becomes a substitute for social activity, particularly in family life. And it offers limited opportunities for direct and immediate dialogue, for although one can discuss what one has seen and heard on television, one has limited opportunities for entering into dialogue with the people on the screen who are addressing one not as an individual but as part of an anonymous audience. One may on rare occasions receive a response to a letter, or even get to meet some television "celebrity"; but communication with most of those seen on the small screen is extremely difficult, and of course, when one talks to the screen, there is no response.

Most religious media critics are also highly critical of the "commercialism" of "popular" television programming. "Listeners and viewers," Fore complains, "increasingly are being treated as commodities rather than as persons."[82] In Hoover's view, "The real buyers in broadcasting are the advertisers, and *their* demands are first in the minds of television entrepreneurs, not those of the viewers, who are the commodity being sold."[83] According to Schultze, "History shows that television quickly became the most thoroughly commercialized mass-communication system in the world."[84] And here religious media critics again find their position supported by secular media critics, particularly those active in the promotion of public, noncommercial broadcasting. Les Brown, in his widely read study of the American television industry, states bluntly that, "The game of television is basically between the network and the advertiser, and the Nielsen digits determine what the latter will pay for the circulation of the commercial."[85] Indeed, "In day-to-day commerce, television is not so much interested in the business of communications as in the business of delivering people to advertisers. People are the merchandise, not the shows. The shows are merely the bait. The consumer, whom the custodians of the medium are pledged to serve, is in fact served up."[86]

Of course, television programming does not have to be largely under the control of big business entrepreneurs and advertisers. In many countries, it is controlled primarily by politicians and bureaucrats, sometimes primarily for propagandist purposes. In theory, it can be under the control of artists or religious leaders or philosophers or the "masses." But in the United States, the land in which the most globally influential forms of television programming have been developed, public, noncommercial television broadcasting, while much praised, has never had more than a small fraction of the cultural impact of its commercial counterpart, despite the warning of high-minded observers that the commercial character of most American television programming has increasingly led to the unwholesome transformation of the entire cultural and social apparatus of the nation through the "merchandising of consciousness."[87]

In a 1938 report on ethical, religious, and social problems posed by the medium of radio, a group of Christian researchers made these keen observations, which apply just as much to television:

Students of society recognize that what is called the "material culture" tends to develop through the multiplication of inventions and the improvement of mechanical processes much more rapidly than does the "adaptive culture"—the means by which society domesticates its new tools and its new toys, making them serve its considered purposes and conserve its higher values. . . . [T]he perfection of material equipment and of mechanical processes is pushed along at high speed by the promise of financial reward, while the building of social controls for the physical, mental, and moral good of the community has no such motivation. This is not to say that those who have an economic stake in an enterprise are without a sense of social responsibility. But it is simple realism to recognize that the ethical controls which prevent an industry from becoming exploitive are not built wholly from within.[88]

These remarks draw our attention to, among other things, the fact that most religious critics of mass media "commercialism" are actually troubled by two distinct aspects of "popular" television programming that are usually but not necessarily combined. The first and more important is an exploitive aspect; whereas authentic culture is, according to traditional understanding, meliorative in nature (or at least in intent), commercial television "culture" generally subordinates, and often sacrifices, the interests of the viewer to the narrower interests of those who determine the form and content of television programming. Whereas the genuine craftsman or professional is essentially concerned with meliorating the condition of his client, patient, student, or customer, and expects only fair remuneration for his work, the manipulative "operator" sees those for whom he practices his "craft" as being essentially means to his own ends.[89] A second aspect is materialism in the form of the commercial television programmer's subordination of spiritual or abstract concerns, like self-improvement and fulfillment of social responsibility, to material concerns, such as the attainment of wealth and the acquisition of property. Of course, one can have nonmaterialistic motives for exploiting one's fellows; one may be interested more in fame or power as such than in wealth and property. But in the television industry, particularly in the United States, manipulativeness and materialism usually go together.

Religious media critics have also expressed concern about what they perceive as a special relationship between television and entertainment. They are aware that some television programs deal with serious and often troubling subject matter, and they know that from its beginnings television has been used in a wide variety of ways by religious leaders and groups, including those seen as representing the theological mainstream of Christianity. Yet they are also aware that given its nature as a medium and its cultural context, television has almost inevitably been turned over largely to entertainment purposes. Most people find their lives difficult and demanding enough apart from television, and they usually prefer television programs that will entertain them and enable them to relax rather than those that will make additional demands on their conscience. Most people watch the occasional documentary program on a social, political, economic, environmental, or medical problem, and there are some people who do prefer such programs to the bland and undemanding fare usually offered on the "tube." But television programming is largely devoted to entertainment, and numerous media critics have lamented that even "serious" programming is regularly reduced to some form of entertainment. Thus, for example, while news broadcasts devote much of their attention to political affairs, they often focus on personalities instead of issues, thereby turning their political coverage into a form of drama; and their coverage of wars and crimes often has the tone and texture of war movies and crime movies. Again, all kinds of "experts" are paraded before the viewer on "talk" shows and information shows, but these "talking heads" have been prepared to make compromises of various sorts in order to be "interesting" to people who do not have the patience to engage in careful, sustained examination of the issues under discussion. Almost inevitably, the simple takes precedence over the complex, and the sensational over the profound. As for religious programming, it has all too often been, in James B. Twitchell's words, "a station on the sideshow, a booth on the midway."[90]

Postman has well articulated the relevant views of many religious media critics. "American television . . . is devoted entirely to supplying its audience with entertainment;"[91] but, "The problem is not that television presents us with entertaining subject matter but that all subject matter is presented as entertaining."[92] That being the case, when television deals with religious subject matter, it can hardly do justice to the complexity of religious spirituality. "[O]n television, religion, like everything else, is presented, quite simply and without apology, as an entertainment. Everything that makes religion an historic, profound and sacred human activity is stripped away; there is no ritual, no dogma, no tradition, no theology, and above all, no sense of spiritual transcendence."[93] Moreover, serious subject matter is transformed by the sea of entertainment programming in which it is submerged, and this is as true of religious programming as of news and documentary programming. "The screen is so saturated with our memories of profane events, so deeply associated with the commercial and entertainment worlds that it is difficult for it to be recreated as a frame for sacred events. Among other things, the viewer is at all times aware that a flick of the switch will produce a different and secular event on the screen—a hockey game, a commercial, a cartoon."[94] Postman acknowledges that spectacle is no stranger to religion itself, with its aesthetic appeal and its rites,[95] but, "The spectacle we find in true religions has as its purpose enchantment, not entertainment. The distinction is critical. By endowing things with magic, enchantment is the means through which we may gain access to sacredness. Entertainment is the means through which we distance ourselves from it."[96]

The rejoinder of those responsible for television programming to criticism is generally the same as most people's response to criticism. If the criticism is perceived as polite and constructive, it is accepted graciously as "something to think about," and if it is regarded as accusatory and severe, it is met with resentment and bewilderment. People who work in the television industry are apt to be less touchy than religious leaders when it is suggested that their vocation requires them to be considerably more competitive than people in most other fields. They may say that they regret the cutthroat competition in their field, but they will probably grant that the various forms of competition—competition for jobs, ratings, prestige, influence, visibility, and indeed professional survival itself—follow naturally from the personalities of the people who enter the profession and the special importance that they attach to their work. If one characterizes them and their line of work as highly competitive, they will likely regard this not as a criticism but as a straightforward and generally accurate description, and some in their field will even regard it as a compliment. In this respect, they tend to differ significantly from most religious leaders and others for whom religious involvement is central to their lives. As a general rule, religionists fail to appreciate the importance of competition in religious life, although this competition manifests itself in numerous ways.[97] Many would take the suggestion that religionists tend to be highly competitive as a charge of hypocrisy.

Nevertheless, those responsible for television programming are likely to be somewhat puzzled when it is suggested that they are involved in a momentous cultural competition with the forces of religion. Perhaps they would have good reason to be puzzled, for while they are probably well aware that television programming is constantly under attack by religious leaders, they do have grounds for believing that they have on the whole been rather conciliatory and even supportive in their dealings with active, highly committed religionists. Many of those involved in the administrative and creative aspects of television programming are, out of personal conviction as well as professional prudence, committed to a liberal attitude toward freedom of expression, including that related to freedom of religion, thought, and conscience. Undoubtedly, many of them are personally religious and raise their families in accordance with traditional religious principles. Even those who are philosophically or ideologically opposed to religion, or at least religion in its conventional or institutional forms, will point to the government regulations and professional codes that, along with prudential considerations, make it extremely difficult for them to promote antireligious propaganda. They could remind religious critics of television of the many kinds of religious programming that are accessible to the viewer, of the favorable publicity that God receives in, say, television movies, situation comedies, talk shows, and interviews with professional athletes, and of how rarely one sees a professed atheist or materialist on such shows, even as a fictional character. And many of them, including those who regard themselves as religious in a conventional way, would even go so far as to say that when they go about performing their professional tasks, they simply do not think much about religion, although they would never consciously do anything to undermine the cultural influence of religion, or anything that could be reasonably viewed as intolerant.

Put on the defensive, they could argue that most people responsible for the television programming in question are basically responding to public demand, and that few people are more sensitive than television programmers to popular taste as indicated by market research and highly developed systems of ratings. (They might point in this regard to the importance of big audiences to advertisers.) They could argue further that prominent religious leaders, who generally appear more frequently on television than secular intellectuals, have often testified to the positive

religious, ethical, and cultural value of certain kinds of television programming. They could insist that television executives have traditionally
been very sensitive to the constructive criticisms of their industry, and
have regularly consulted major religious organizations for guidance on
how television programming can be improved.

They might well be moved to point out that religious and other ostensibly high-minded critics of television programming often send inconsistent messages to the industry. On one hand, broadcasters are
regularly criticized for putting out so much junk and fluff, programs that
are lightweight, unimaginative, and unchallenging. Yet when these
broadcasters try to offer programming that is serious, provocative, and
controversial, they are often criticized for being arrogant, self-important,
and manipulative, and for overreaching and attempting to usurp the
roles of their betters in religion, education, the humanities, and the fine
arts. The religious media theorist, A. William Bluem, has acknowledged
the difficulty of their situation:

[T]he broadcaster is increasingly conscious of the fact that every move he makes
has widespread, though immeasurable social influence and impact. Unlike the
churchman, however, the broadcaster in quest of social relevance is more often
scorned for what he *is* doing rather than for what he fails to do. He operates in
the classic do-and-be-damned-don't-and-be-damned mode. He is encouraged to
editorialize—to have the courage to ignore "pressure" and to lead, and at the
same time asked to be "fair" to all points of view. He is asked to reflect the
political life of our society, and then condemned for turning politics into a
"show." He is asked to set forth the raw and real confrontations of our time,
and then flayed for "creating demagogues" and "sensationalizing" his reports
of our social ills and conflicts. He is asked to entertain and delight—to lift, with
laughter and escape, the burdens of a tired and driven society and he is promptly
castigated for not being "serious."[98]

Bluem further notes that even when construed narrowly, the broadcaster's obligations to religious communities are not particularly clear:

In the dialogue between church and broadcasting, the principal concerns of the
broadcaster are: (1) What policies should he adopt regarding the assignment of
air time to the multiplicity of different religious groups and organizations? and
(2) Beyond his own recognition of community religious needs, what is required
of him by law and by regulative directive? In neither of these aspects of his day-
to-day decision-making are the answers clear, and operators of TV and radio
stations are fully aware that errors in judgment may create severe difficulties for
them.[99]

Tired of being browbeaten by religious media critics that they regard
as smugly self-righteous and self-serving, those responsible for television

programming may want to go on the offensive. They can begin by ar-
guing that the fundamental competition that television gives the forces
of religion is wholly natural, and not essentially different from the sort
of competition given to religion by philosophers, writers, artists, politicians, secular educators, or for that matter, anyone whose work shifts
the attention of individuals and society away from the agenda of religious leaders and groups. Such competition is not essentially unfair, and
the mass media may receive an undue amount of criticism merely because they are so successful and so well received. Moreover, competition
is not in itself a bad thing; humanists, social scientists, and even religious
thinkers have acknowledged the positive value of fair competition,[100] and
in the United States, vigorous competition is often associated with "the
American way." Again, whereas most religionists are tied to a particular
denomination,[101] a community of believers with a distinctive worldview,
television programmers on the major networks make an effort to be inclusive in a manner appropriate to an institution that serves a pluralistic
society. It is noteworthy that the long history of interdenominational and
intradenominational competition throughout the world, as well as the
war of religious leaders against secularism and "free thought," is marked
by countless examples of unfair competition, many of which have involved the murder, torture, silencing, and oppression of idealistic, creative individuals and masses of innocents.[102] The proverbial "glass
house" of religious media critics is out there for all open-minded students of history to observe.

Continuing on the offensive, defenders of television programming
may want to scrutinize the claims of those defenders of religion who
believe that religious agencies alone can satisfactorily perform certain
fundamental cultural functions. For one thing, the respect that religionists themselves have for the value of television is evidenced not only by
the praise that they sometimes bestow upon some nonreligious television
programming, but by their eagerness to make more and more use of a
form of technology that they periodically pooh-pooh as being intrinsically vitiated by its commercialism, tendency to promote passivity, and
emphasis on entertainment. Second, while religion, with its rituals and
unique forms of myth and symbolism, is undoubtedly a distinctive form
of experience and culture,[103] it long before the invention of television lost
its status as the unrivaled authority on moral, metaphysical, scientific,
aesthetic, and educational matters, having been successfully challenged
and transformed by the forces of reason and creativity. But most importantly, its competence at performing certain fundamental cultural functions can itself be called into question.

Consider first the role of religious institutions to inform and provide
general knowledge. The record here is clearly a mixed one, as exempli-
fied by the fact that the great church that in the medieval period pro-

vided the world with its first great universities also bequeathed to it a form of systematic misinformation (and indeed a name for it, *propaganda*)[104] and the most notorious institution ever founded for the suppression of freedom of thought, conscience, and expression, the Inquisition. While some of the world's greatest teachers have been religious thinkers and scholars, there are now as ever fanatics and crackpots of all faiths promoting outrageous ideas about everything from evolution, sex, and the impending end of the world to what people of rival faiths believe. World religions have certainly captured important myths and heroes, but they have also led their followers to ignore and undervalue others; and for all the fine role models that they have held up to their followers, they have also heaped praise on some strange "saints" like Simon Stylites, whose name is derived in part from the fact that he spent much of his life on a column, on which he practiced bizarre "mortifications."[105] World religions have unquestionably provided people with unique forms of hope, compassion, and peace of mind, and with guidance on how to cope with the trials of life. But they have also given rise to a great deal of morbidity and left many of their less stable followers sick with guilt, fear, and frustration. Sigmund Freud, for one, was not favorably impressed by the rich fantasy world of the major Western faiths, and in an important passage in *The Future of an Illusion*, he observes:

Religion has clearly performed great services for human civilization. It has contributed much towards the taming of the asocial instincts. But not enough. It has ruled human society for many thousands of years and has had time to show what it can achieve. If it had succeeded in making the majority of mankind happy, in comforting them, in reconciling them to life and in making them into vehicles of civilization, no one would dream of attempting to alter the existing conditions. But what do we see instead? We see that an appallingly large number of people are dissatisfied with civilization and unhappy in it, and feel it as a yoke which must be shaken off; and that these people either do everything in their power to change that civilization, or else go so far in their hostility to it that they will have nothing to do with civilization or with a restriction of instinct.[106]

Freud undoubtedly said many foolish things about religion, as other depth psychologists like Alfred Adler and Carl Jung were quick to point out, but the insights embodied in the passage here quoted should not be taken lightly.

World religions have certainly given countless people a sense of belonging, as a community of believers is ordinarily one of the most important to which an individual can belong, and they have provided countless societies with stability. But as they have given people a sense of belonging, they have given some a sense of being excluded. To belong to a denominational or intradenominational group is necessarily to be an outsider to others; and interdenominational and intradenominational rivalries and conflicts have led not only to invidious distinctions that breed frustration and resentment but to hatred, violence, and wars that represent instability of the worst kind.

Defenders and promoters of religion have plenty to answer for, and despite what many of them would have us believe, the mass media, including television, have for the most part given them a free ride and failed to call them to order. The forum that has been so regularly provided to the likes of Jimmy Swaggart, Jerry Falwell, and Donald E. Wildmon has been rather more sparingly offered to people like Bertrand Russell, Paul Kurtz, and Kai Nielsen. Baseball players, Hollywood starlets, pop psychologists, and rock "musicians" get a great deal more airtime than serious religious thinkers and teachers, but thoughtful critics of religion and the dominant Western faiths get even less airtime than neo-Nazi hatemongers and people who claim that they have discovered a cure for baldness. But we have not yet considered what many would regard as the crux of the matter in making a utilitarian assessment of the comparative value of the cultural impact of religion and television, for thus far we have only indirectly considered the matter of moral education, and which of the two teaches moral lessons better, more effectively evokes moral criticism, better helps people to recognize the inadequacies of the moral world, and does more to promote salutary social activism.

This may indeed be the crux of the matter, but anyone with even a purely intuitive understanding of the complexity of a philosophical problem will appreciate how little is to be gained by trying to calculate— applying arbitrary numbers to items arbitrarily selected for inclusion on lists of supposedly outstanding or paradigmatic cases—how much more effective religion has been than television as a field or instrument for moral education. Besides, as a form of culture and a phenomenon that exerts influence upon culture, television is in its infancy in comparison with religion, which as a form of experience and culture may perhaps be said to predate rationality itself. The disparity in historical depth, development, and influence makes a comparative assessment here seem unlikely to yield useful insights. And if the utilitarian assessment of television is necessarily highly subjective and influenced by all sorts of determining factors, the assessment of religion as such is notoriously so, and involves the most existential form of commitment of which a human being is capable. Although we shall later consider how television and religion relate as forms of experience and culture, we should not deceive ourselves into believing that assessing the value of religion or even television as a moral educator is a more or less objective matter of gathering data and weighing the results by ordinary criteria.

Consider in this regard the conflicting opinions of three of the most interesting of all cultural theorists. Freud, while granting that religion has "contributed much towards the taming of the asocial instincts," believes nevertheless that religious teachings are "neurotic relics,"[107] and that only when human beings are capable of surmounting the "infantilism" of commitment to the religious "illusion" will they be ready for "education to reality."[108] However, on the basis of historical analyses, Christopher Dawson, the Christian historian and philosopher of culture, concludes that, "The whole history of culture shows that man has a natural tendency to seek a religious foundation for his social way of life and that when culture loses its spiritual basis it becomes unstable. Nothing has occurred to alter these facts."[109] Moreover,

We are only just beginning to understand how intimately and profoundly the vitality of a society is bound up with its religion. It is the religious impulse which supplies the cohesive force which unifies a society and a culture. The great civilisations of the world do not produce the great religions as a kind of cultural by-product; in a very real sense, the great religions are the foundations on which the great civilisations rest. A society which has lost its religion becomes sooner or later a society which has lost its culture.[110]

And Friedrich Nietzsche, avoiding both extreme positions, suggests that, "The selective and cultivating influence, always destructive as well as creative and form-giving, which can be exerted with the help of religions, is always multiple and different according to the sort of human beings who are placed under its spell and protection."[111]

In any case, those responsible for popular television programming who find themselves confronted with an onslaught of criticism from self-righteous religious media critics could point out that the most fundamental charges that have been directed against them have been directed at religious leaders as well. Nietzsche, although his views on religion were complex and multifaceted, never ceased to be impressed by what he took to be the passivity engendered by Christianization:

One should not embellish or dress up Christianity: it has waged a *war to the death* against [the] *higher* type of man, it has excommunicated all the fundamental instincts of this type, it has distilled evil, the *Evil One*, out of these instincts—the strong human being as the type of reprehensibility, as the "outcast." Christianity has taken the side of everything weak, base, ill-constituted, it has made an ideal out of *opposition* to the preservative instincts of strong life; it has depraved the reason even of the intellectually strongest natures by teaching men to feel the supreme values of intellectuality as sinful, as misleading, as *temptations*.[112]

It may be then that religion, or at least the predominant type of Christian religion, long before television made the masses even more passive, had gone a long way toward turning them into manipulable sheep. If Nietzsche is right, then, "From the start, the Christian Faith is a sacrifice: a sacrifice of all freedom, all pride, all self-confidence of the spirit; at the same time, enslavement and self-mockery."[113]

With respect to the matter of commercialism, here again, religion, despite its special involvement with spirituality, is not immune to thoughtful criticism of a kind that is routinely directed against popular television programming. The alliances between powerful business and political interests and their ecclesiastical or denominational counterparts are widely known. It should not take much imagination to realize that all sorts of religious functionaries, and their associates in various secular fields, have a vested interest in the survival and promotion of established religious institutions. To put the point more bluntly, one could say that religion itself is very much a business, and countless religious "authorities" of one or another order of importance derive income, eminence, and influence from their position. It is indeed striking that religious competition is in many ways like economic competition, and can be understood by means of models routinely applied to the analysis of economic competition.[114] Over the centuries, religious reformers have bitterly complained about the exploitation of innocents by cynical ecclesiastical and denominational manipulators; they have denounced everything from allowing the temple to be turned into a den of thieves[115] to the selling of indulgences, and they have condemned bishops and televangelists alike for amassing material wealth at the expense of their flock.

In "cultivating" passivity in the masses, venal religious leaders are not unlike those television programmers who seek to reduce viewers to mindless consumers. John M. Phelan has usefully observed that, "Missionary Christianity, which exported . . . cultural automatisms to the wide world, anticipated the 'global reach' of Coca-colonization and contemporary 'information imperialism' of the multinational communication conglomerates."[116] Television itself reveals how close the Christian proselytizer can be to the advertiser of material goods: "Both commercial traders and Christian missionaries are enthralled by the electronic potential for 'outreach.' Their focus is on reaching millions and millions with an identical cassetted format."[117] For the student of cultural criticism, it is particularly noteworthy that, "The standard bemoanings of mass culture found in thinkers as diverse and divergent as Herbert Marcuse, Gabriel Marcel, Dwight Macdonald and Hans Magnus Enzensberger were all antedated centuries ago by the elitist criticisms of Erasmus, Thomas More, and other deplorers of what John Colet, their contemporary, called 'mechanical Christianity.' The history of Christianity as a mass movement is replete with all the devices of automatism that bolster authoritarianism."[118]

Of course, no one could make much of a case for the thesis that religion is essentially a matter of entertainment. Even so, when Postman contrasts Christian television programming (and television programming in general) with Christianity as such, a "demanding and serious religion,"[119] he may be overstating his point. The Christianity of Simon Stylites, or for that matter of Roger Williams, Albert Schweitzer, and Dietrich Bonhoeffer, is a far cry from that of the overwhelming majority of those people who have generally been regarded as Christians, people whose involvement with the rituals and ceremonies of the ancient faith falls considerably short of qualifying as "enchantment."[120] "Popular" religion is in some ways closer to popular television programming than it is to "demanding and serious" religion; it is often little more than an occasion for socializing, having a few drinks, and enjoying the "show."

You will perhaps have noticed by now that in all of this severe criticism of the darker side of religion, those responsible for television programming have themselves not been heard from. Generally, these people, even when they have responded forcefully to those religious media critics that they regard as dangerous reactionaries, have opted for what they take to be the prudent response to religious media criticism. "A soft answer turneth away wrath: but grievous words stir up anger."[121] The wrath of the self-righteous is not easily mollified; but often the promise to reform, delivered in a subservient or obsequious manner, will keep them quiet for a while. Besides, many television programmers are religious people themselves and thus disinclined to take the offensive against religious media critics. And undoubtedly many television programmers believe that the criticisms of their religious competitors are not worth answering, especially since these competitors are fighting a losing battle. Again, few of the people responsible for television programming know enough about cultural theory, much less philosophy of religion, to have something useful to contribute to this kind of analysis.

There is no dearth of media critics—professional and amateur, high-minded and self-serving, informed and ignorant. Over a decade ago, Phelan could point to "over 500 organized groups concerned with the moral obligations of the broadcast industry and the moral tone of broadcast programming."[122] Most of these groups he regarded as "special interest groups dedicated to ensuring that their constituents are fairly represented on the media and/or equally hired by the media."[123] But he also acknowledged the existence of at least twenty groups, some affiliated with churches, "whose interest in the media is not confined to its service of a special interest."[124] Media criticism has, if anything, increased since Phelan made these observations, though perhaps these days he would be less inclined to make a sharp distinction between special interest groups and others. In fact, it is becoming increasingly inappropriate to make a sharp distinction between high-minded media critics and self-serving ones or between informed and ignorant ones; and often it is even difficult to distinguish between the professionals and the amateurs.

There are, in any case, all sorts of media critics, and they have rather different concerns, motives, and objectives. Some, Phelan observed, are "conservative," and others are "quasi-revolutionary and anti-capitalist."[125] Evaluative positions on the mass media ordinarily reflect evaluative positions on mass culture in general, and Michael R. Real has observed that among the holders of the latter are liberal apologists; empirical, descriptive, or historical "objectivists"; progressive elitists; traditional elitists; cultural separatist radicals; and Marxist structural radicals.[126] We have also seen that media critics and general cultural critics may attach any degree of positive or negative value to the cultural role of religion.

Journalism scholar James B. Lemert has warned that "media criticism doesn't exist in a vacuum. It is written by critics who have a particular purpose or point of view and it is directed to a particular audience."[127] There is value in this caveat, but some media critics have more than one purpose, and some have only the vaguest idea of who or what their audience will be. Furthermore, the various purposes or points of view that different media critics have should not all be seen in the same light or treated with the same degree of respect.

People write and talk about television because they believe that the subject is worth writing and talking about and because they believe that there are people who will be interested in their ideas on the subject. Indeed many people are interested in the subject of television, which is hardly surprising, for many people spend a considerable amount of time watching television. Those who do not are usually well aware that their own lives and the character of society are significantly influenced by the ideas, attitudes, and behavior of the many people who do. Even most of those individuals not given to reflection on television and its cultural or anticultural impact would probably allow that such reflection can be of great practical value; many of them could probably even be persuaded that television can be an appropriate subject for abstract, theoretical, intellectual reflection.

Religion is almost universally regarded as an appropriate subject for both practical and intellectual reflection, and people who are interested in religion have plenty to think about. Such people may well be interested in television on its own account. But most of these people will be interested in television partly because of the various relationships between television and religion. For example, as Hoover has observed,

One way of seeing the theological challenge of television [and related media] . . . is to realize that it is through these technologies that a major portion of our society's claim on us and on our time and commitments takes place. I am not saying television is an instrument of the devil. Neither am I saying that these technologies are somehow theologically or ethically neutral. They are, by virtue of their particular place in the social, economic, and intellectual life of our culture the means by which the demands of earth are made to press on us. As such, they take on a theological dimension which involves our being careful, circumspect, and temperate in our use of them. At times we should stand, with Elijah, and call to accountability these institutions that have come to stand so much for mercenary, vainglorious secularism in our society. . . . Media awareness is no longer a luxury, an affectation, or a hobby. It is now part of adult basic education. In the future, no one who wishes to develop expertise in the disciplines of teaching, ministry, counseling, or even parenting will be able to consider themselves prepared unless they have also dealt with the development of basic media awareness, consumption, and advocacy skills.[128]

As for religion itself, no one seriously interested in culture can afford to ignore it as a subject for close investigation. From the saint and the fanatic to the philosophical materialist and the venal television programmer, everybody is influenced by religion, if only in obscure and indirect ways; and the obscure and indirect ways can sometimes be the most consequential. So if there are tensions in our society between the forces of religion and the forces of television, then whether they are appropriately characterized as competitive or in some other way, they are for both practical and intellectual reasons worthy of close consideration by students of culture, including humanists. Understanding them can be of service to us in our endeavors to be socially responsible and to contribute to the melioration of the cultural life of our society. And reflection on culture in general, while valuable for many reasons, is perhaps most important because it provides us with insights into ourselves as individuals, and specifically, into how we came to be the individuals that we are. In this sense, what Michael R. Real says of mass-mediated culture applies to all culture, that to investigate it is "to apply the ancient directive of Socrates: Know thyself."[129]

NOTES TO CHAPTER 1

1. *The Oxford English Dictionary* (1933), II.

2. Cf. Jay Newman, *Competition in Religious Life*, Editions SR, Vol. 11 (Waterloo, ON: Wilfrid Laurier University Press, 1989), pp. 5–39.

3. Robert S. Alley, *Television: Ethics for Hire?* (Nashville: Abingdon, 1977), p. 23.

4. William F. Fore, *Television and Religion: The Shaping of Faith, Values, and Culture* (Minneapolis: Augsburg, 1987), pp. 11–12.

5. Ibid., p. 24.

6. William Kuhns, *The Electronic Gospel: Religion and the Media* (New York: Herder and Herder, 1969), p. 10.

7. Ibid., p. 163.

8. David Porter, *The Media: A Christian Point of View* (London: Scripture Union, 1974), pp. 55–56.

9. Donald E. Wildmon, *The Home Invaders* (Wheaton, IL: SP Publications, 1985), p. 5.

10. Steven Starker, *Evil Influences: Crusades against the Mass Media* (New Brunswick, NJ: Transaction Publishers, 1989), p. 181.

11. "In Conversation: Paul Kurtz, International Humanist and Ethical Union," interview by Robert Abelman, in Robert Abelman and Stewart M. Hoover, eds., *Religious Television: Controversies and Conclusions* (Norwood, NJ: Ablex, 1990), p. 153.

12. Herbert I. Schiller, *Culture, Inc.: The Corporate Takeover of Public Expression* (New York: Oxford University Press, 1989), p. 17.

13. Ibid., pp. 90–91.

14. Gregor T. Goethals, *The TV Ritual: Worship at the Video Altar* (Boston: Beacon Press, 1980), ch. 4.

15. Ibid., p. 2.

16. John M. Phelan, *Disenchantment: Meaning and Morality in the Media* (New York: Hastings House, 1980), p. 148.

17. Quentin J. Schultze, *Television: Manna from Hollywood?* (Grand Rapids, MI: Zondervan, 1986), p. 19. Cf. Quentin J. Schultze, "Television as a Sacred Text," in John P. Ferré, ed., *Channels of Belief: Religion and American Commercial Television* (Ames: Iowa State University Press, 1990), pp. 3–27.

18. Stewart M. Hoover, *Mass Media Religion: The Social Sources of the Electronic Church* (Newbury Park, CA: Sage Publications, 1988), p. 241.

19. Ibid.

20. Neil Postman, *Amusing Ourselves to Death: Public Discourse in the Age of Show Business* (New York: Viking, 1985), p. 118.

21. Ibid., p. 87.

22. Ibid., p. 119.

23. Ibid., p. 123.

24. Ibid., p. 159.

25. Peter G. Horsfield, *Religious Television: The American Experience* (New York: Longmans, 1984), p. 68.

26. Ibid., p. 69.

27. Quentin Schultze, *Televangelism and American Culture: The Business of Popular Religion* (Grand Rapids, MI: Baker Book House, 1991), p. 119.

28. Schultze, *Television: Manna from Hollywood?*, p. 155.

29. Hoover, *Mass Media Religion*, p. 237.

30. Stephen R. Lawhead, *Turn Back the Night* (Westchester, IL: Crossway Books, 1985), p. 5.

31. Ibid., p. 57.

32. Hoover, *Mass Media Religion*, p. 224.

33. Porter, *The Media*, pp. 49–50.

34. Schultze, *Television: Manna from Hollywood?*, p. 8.

35. Ibid., pp. 9, 11.

36. Marshall McLuhan, *Understanding Media: The Extensions of Man* (New York: New American Library, 1964), p. 32.

37. Ibid., p. 36.

38. Ibid., pp. 55–56.

39. Ibid., p. 60.

40. Ibid., p. 64.

41. Gunnar Andrén, *Media and Morals: The Rationality of Mass Rhetoric and the Autonomy of the Individual* (Stockholm: Akademilitteratur, 1978), pp. 5–6.

42. McLuhan, *Understanding Media*, p. 289.

43. Ibid., p. 292. Cf. pp. 272–74.

44. Ibid., p. 294. Cf. pp. 269–72.

45. Ibid., p. 286.

46. Postman, *Amusing Ourselves to Death*, pp. 8–10.

47. Ibid., p. 8.

48. Ibid., p. 10.

49. Ibid., p. 92.

50. Martin H. Seiden, *Access to the American Mind: The Impact of the New Mass Media* (New York: Shapolsky, 1991), p. 223.

51. Dennis Howitt, *The Mass Media and Social Problems* (Oxford: Pergamon, 1982), p. 67.

52. Ibid., p. 6.

53. Horsfield, *Religious Television*, p. 136.

54. Schultze, *Television: Manna from Hollywood?*, p. 12.

55. Porter, *The Media*, p. 55.

56. Schultze, *Televangelism*, p. 248.

57. Starker, *Evil Influences*, p. 14.

58. Schultze, *Television: Manna from Hollywood?*, p. 8.

59. Steve Bruce, *Pray TV: Televangelism in America* (London: Routledge, 1990), pp. 117–18.

60. Starker, *Evil Influences*, p. 6.

61. Cf. Fore, *Television and Religion*, pp. 11–12.

62. Ibid., pp. 67–70.

63. Porter, *The Media*, p. 50.

64. Schultze, *Television: Manna from Hollywood?*, p. 137.

65. Fore, *Television and Religion*, pp. 19–20.

66. Alley, *Television: Ethics for Hire?*, p. 133.

67. Henry J. Perkinson, *Getting Better: Television and Moral Progress* (New Brunswick, NJ: Transaction Publishers, 1991), p. 9.

68. Starker, *Evil Influences*, p. 140.

69. McLuhan, *Understanding Media*, p. 267.

70. Michael R. Real, *Mass-Mediated Culture* (Englewood Cliffs, NJ: Prentice-Hall, 1977), p. viii.

71. Alley, *Television: Ethics for Hire?*, pp. 164–65.

72. Ibid., p. 133.

73. Wildmon, *The Home Invaders*, pp. 36–37.

74. Postman, *Amusing Ourselves to Death*, p. 121.

75. Porter, *The Media*, p. 51.

76. Ibid., p. 52.

77. Real, *Mass-Mediated Culture*, p. 10.

78. Ibid., p. 199.

79. Ibid., pp. 264–70.

80. Schultze, *Television: Manna from Hollywood?*, p. 146.

81. Ibid., p. 151.

82. Fore, *Television and Religion*, p. 31.

83. Stewart M. Hoover, *The Electronic Giant: A Critique of the Telecommunications Revolution from a Christian Perspective* (Elgin, IL: The Brethren Press, 1982), p. 40.

84. Schultze, *Television: Manna from Hollywood?*, p. 12.

85. Les Brown, *Television: The Business Behind the Box* (New York: Harcourt Brace Jovanovich, 1971), p. 15.

86. Ibid., pp. 15–16.

87. *A Public Trust: The Report of the Carnegie Commission on the Future of Public Broadcasting* (New York: Bantam Books, 1979), p. 296.

88. Department of Research and Education of the Federal Council of the Churches of Christ in America, *Broadcasting and the Public: A Case Study in Social Ethics* (New York: Abingdon, 1938), pp. 181–82.

89. Cf. Plato *Republic* 336B–347E.

90. James B. Twitchell, *Carnival Culture: The Trashing of Taste in America* (New York: Columbia University Press, 1992), p. 243.

91. Postman, *Amusing Ourselves to Death*, p. 87.

92. Ibid.

93. Ibid., pp. 116–17.

94. Ibid., pp. 119–20.

95. Ibid., p. 122.

96. Ibid.

97. Cf. Newman, *Competition in Religious Life*.

98. A. William Bluem, *Religious Television Programs: A Study of Relevance* (New York: Hastings House, 1969), pp. 10–11.

99. Ibid., p. 12.

100. Cf. Newman, *Competition in Religious Life*, pp. 45–48.

101. Ibid., pp. 53–100, 198–202.

102. Ibid., pp. 55–100, 148–66, 192–98.

103. Cf., for example, R. G. Collingwood, *Speculum Mentis* (Oxford: Clarendon Press, 1924), ch. 4; Ernst Cassirer, *An Essay on Man* (New Haven, CT: Yale University Press, 1944), ch. 7.

104. The term is derived from a word in the Latin name for the Congregation for the Propagation of the Faith, the *Congregatio de Propaganda Fide*.

105. Cf., for example, Omer Englebert, *The Lives of the Saints* (1951), trans. Christopher and Anne Fremantle (New York: Collier Books, 1964), p. 23.

106. Sigmund Freud, *The Future of an Illusion* (1927), trans. W. D. Robson-Scott (1953), revised and newly ed. James Strachey (1961) (Garden City, NY: Doubleday, 1964), pp. 60–61.

107. Ibid., p. 72.

108. Ibid., p. 81.

109. Christopher Dawson, *Religion and Culture* (New York: Sheed and Ward, 1948), p. 217.

110. Christopher Dawson, "Religion and the Life of Civilisation," in *Enquiries into Religion and Culture* (New York: Sheed and Ward, 1933), p. 115.

111. Friedrich Nietzsche, *Beyond Good and Evil* (1886), sec. 61, trans. Walter Kaufmann (New York: Vintage Books, 1966), p. 72.

112. Friedrich Nietzsche, *The Anti-Christ* (1895; written in 1888), sec. 5, trans. R. J. Hollingdale (London: Penguin Books, 1990 [1968]), p. 127.

113. Cf. Nietzsche, *Beyond Good and Evil*, sec. 46; op. cit., p. 60.

114. Cf. Newman, *Competition in Religious Life*, pp. 140–46.

115. Matthew 21:12–15; Mark 11:15–18.

116. Phelan, *Disenchantment*, p. 148.

117. Ibid., p. 150.

118. Ibid., p. 148.

119. Postman, *Amusing Ourselves to Death*, p. 121.

120. Ibid., p. 122.

121. Proverbs 15:1.

122. Phelan, *Disenchantment*, p. 51.

123. Ibid.

124. Ibid.

125. Ibid., p. 53.

126. Real, *Mass-Mediated Culture*, p. 16.

127. James B. Lemert, *Criticizing the Media: Empirical Approaches* (Newbury Park, CA: Sage Publications, 1989), p. 25.

128. Hoover, *The Electronic Giant*, pp. 154–55.

129. Real, *Mass-Mediated Culture*, p. 6.

CHAPTER TWO

Competition Between Religion and Television: Motives and Strategies

In working to understand better the competition between religion and television, we need to remember that though religion and television, as phenomena, can be conceived as impersonal abstractions, as cultural products they can be fully understood only in relation to the ideas, values, motives, and aspirations of the people who have been responsible for their creation, development, adaptation, utilization, and promotion. Thus when the subject of competition between religion and television arises, it is useful to consider who represents religion and television and what objects these people are competing for. Not surprisingly, in the various competitions between the forces of religion and the forces of television, different groups of religionists and "television people" are doing the competing. Also, while *competition* is not a technical term and is used in everyday discourse, a more definite conception of competition not only would be generally enlightening but might lead to recognition that certain cases are not genuine competition at all.

We shall soon be turning our attention to such matters. It will help if we first examine a controversial and quite unsatisfactory account of what is taken in certain circles to be the paradigmatic and most critically important form of competition between religion and television. This account involves a "conspiracy theory" according to which secular humanists in the United States and certain other Western societies are deliberately and surreptitiously making use of television in order to undermine the Christian cultural foundations of those societies. It has been promoted by many people associated with the "religious right" and with conservative ideology. If this theory has received more attention than it deserves, it is because of its sensationalistic flavor, because of the visibility and shrillness of its promoters, and because people active in the mass media draw attention to it in order to make religious media critics look worse than most really are and to deflect attention away from reasoned, disciplined, religious media criticism that is not so easily countered.

We shall focus here on a version of the account offered by Donald E. Wildmon,[1] who for a time was turned by functionaries in the mass media into something of a celebrity, and whose indiscriminate broadsides against the American television industry have done considerable damage to the cause of serious religious media critics. We will not be interested here so much in the account itself as in what the inadequacies of such an account indirectly reveal about steps that ought to be taken to understand the principal forms of competition between religion and television. The version of the account that we will be considering is not significantly better or worse than most accounts of competition between religion and television that are based on the conspiracy theory; but while representative in this sense, it has received more attention than any version of the account since that promulgated in England in the 1960s by Mary Whitehouse.[2]

Wildmon's 1985 book, *The Home Invaders*, represents something of a program statement. It hardly represents Wildmon's last word on the subjects addressed, and he may have significantly altered some of his views since he wrote this book. Some of his points would seem stronger if supported by the arguments and research studies that he, his associates, and certain other observers have made since *The Home Invaders* appeared in print. Nevertheless, the strongly polemic and uncompromising character of the work, combined with its influence and value as a program statement, makes it an appropriate specimen for the kind of exposition and evaluation that students of the humanities are routinely engaged in.

The back cover of Wildmon's *The Home Invaders* tells us that the author "pastored in the United Methodist Church for thirteen years before founding the National Federation for Decency in 1977. He has appeared on numerous television shows, including *Donahue*, *Nightline*, *The Today Show*, and *Good Morning America*, and he has also been featured in *TV Guide*, *The Saturday Evening Post*, and the major news magazines. Wildmon, his wife Lynda, and their four children live in Tupelo, Mississippi." This blurb is revealing on several levels. It tells us first that the author is by vocation essentially a "pastor," and this designation is itself rather interesting. On the positive side, it recalls Jesus' moving description of himself as "the good shepherd":

I am the good shepherd: the good shepherd giveth his life for the sheep. But he that is an hireling, and not the shepherd, whose own the sheep are not, seeth the wolf coming, and leaveth the sheep, and fleeth: and the wolf catcheth them, and scattereth the sheep. The hireling fleeth, because he is an hireling, and careth not for the sheep. I am the good shepherd, and know my sheep, and am known of mine. As the Father knoweth me, even so know I the Father: and I lay down my life for the sheep.[3]

Pastor Wildmon, having seen the mass media "wolf" coming, is not one to flee; and he is prepared to give a substantial part of his life to protecting the flock from the corrupting influence of the wolf. But there is a negative side to this image of the pastor, especially in relation to those who have not demonstrated, in the great tradition of Christian martyrs, that they are prepared to lay down their lives for the sheep. It is well characterized in part by Thrasymachus in Plato's *Republic* when he ridicules Socrates for undervaluing the self-serving aspect of the shepherd's work:

"[Y]ou fancy that the shepherd or neatherd fattens or tends the sheep or oxen with a view to their own good and not to the good of himself or his master; and you further imagine that the rulers of states, if they are true rulers, never think of their subjects as sheep, and that they are not studying their own advantage day and night.[4]

Socrates has a wise rejoinder to this point,[5] and one that foreshadows authentic New Testament teaching; but the fact remains that the shepherd who fails to appreciate his status as a craftsman can easily end up simply exploiting his flock, just fleeing the sheep and fattening them up for someone's dinner table. Moreover, the pastor who looks after a human flock must think very highly of himself to feel it appropriate for him to look after the interests of those who are not virtuous enough to be able to look after their own interests.

Neither is Wildmon's denominational affiliation insignificant. He pastored in a particular church, the United Methodist Church, and though he goes on in *The Home Invaders* and elsewhere to speak for and to the majority of decent Americans and decent Christians, the fact is that the United Methodist Church, like all denominations, has distinctive theological and ethical orientations that are not entirely shared by most other Christian denominations, much less by Americans who are not Christians. There are undoubtedly significant limits to the degree to which a United Methodist minister from Tupelo, Mississippi, can understand, sympathize with, and represent the worldviews of American Christians of other denominations and theological and ethical orientations, or the worldviews of the many Americans who are not even Christians.

The name of Wildmon's organization and the circumstances of its founding also give us food for thought. The term *decency* has come in everyday English to be notably ambiguous. It can still have a lofty significance, but unlike such terms as *goodness, compassion,* and *integrity,* it often carries with it the suggestion of the user's self-righteousness and excessive concern with secondary moral vices, particularly those related to sexual behavior. Quentin J. Schultze may well have Christian defenders of "decency" in mind when he criticizes his fellow Christian media critics with the observation that,

We err, however, by limiting morality to sex, violence, and profanity. Sexually related sins are not necessarily more severe than others. Our prudishness is evident in our frequent preoccupation with human sexuality and our relative disregard for sins related to greed, covetousness, and injustice. Television's general moral climate is far more evil than the few sexually explicit scenes would make us believe. What about lying, cheating, and stealing? What about disrespect for legitimate authority? What about racism and sexism?[6]

In fact, in his concern for "decency," Wildmon appears to be rather more concerned with the evils of pornography and homosexuality than with the evils of economic exploitation, racism, and sexism, and in this way, among others, he fails to rise to the level of moral vision that has been attained by more thoughtful Christians, including those in the United Methodist Church. Moreover, it is interesting that Wildmon is said in the blurb to have founded his organization, for this suggests that despite his respect on several levels for both traditional ecclesiastical authority and the value of cooperation, Wildmon is somewhat lacking in confidence in the competence of ecclesiastical establishments and of those who might have lent prestige and weight to his organization by serving as co-founders.

But perhaps the most striking feature of the blurb is the remarkable authority it assigns to some of the very television programs (and indirectly, television executives) that Wildmon condemns in the book for moral bankruptcy—in particular, "talk" shows and news and information programs. The citation of the *Donahue* show is especially interesting in light of the fact that this program has been regularly criticized for sensationalism and for preoccupation with strange sexual behavior. Wildmon and his publishers and editors have failed to appreciate the irony of more importance being attached to his having appeared on numerous shows of the kind that he sharply censures than to his educational attainments, his charitable works, and the praise he has elicited from respected religious leaders and scholars. This may not be outright hypocrisy, but it is rather curious.

We noted in Chapter 1 Wildmon's core position:

The organized church in America faces the greatest threat to its existence since our country was founded. . . . There is an intentional effort among many of the leaders of our media to reshape our society, to replace the Christian view of man as our foundation with the humanist view of man.[7]

Wildmon sees many "leaders of our media" as representing the competitors of the forces of sound religion, and he explicitly states that theirs is an "intentional effort" to reshape our society by replacing basic Christian conceptions with non-Christian and indeed anti-Christian "humanist" conceptions. (When Wildmon speaks of "humanism" here, he specifically has in mind secular humanism as opposed to the types of humanism that have been embraced by certain thinkers in the mainstream of Christian theology and philosophy.) Somewhat misleadingly, Wildmon characterizes secular humanism as itself conveying a kind of religious message, one that conflicts with traditional Christian teaching.[8]

Wildmon's points in defense of his core position are succinctly conveyed by some of the titles he provides for sections of the book: "No Positive Portrayal of Christians;"[9] "Children Told to Help Conquer Forces of Good;"[10] "Humanist Values Presented in Best Possible Light;"[11] and so forth. Not all of Wildmon's points are implausible, but the stronger among them are lost in a sea of overgeneralization and paranoia, and the evils that he ignores or undervalues are, on balance, at least as important as those that he uncovers.

Wildmon realizes that he is for the most part preaching to the converted, but he is trying to stimulate his readers to be more active in their response to the mass media wolf. Accordingly, he indicates for his readers the "long-range actions needed,"[12] and he maintains, despite criticism of his organization by professed liberals and some others, that boycotting is not "censorship" but rather "stewardship."[13] At the end of chapters in the book, Wildmon presents what he calls "discussion and reflection questions"; these questions are leading and manipulative in that their aim is not to elicit genuine weighing of alternative possible answers but to reinforce the messages that he has been sending. I list below some of these questions; and those that I have marked with an asterisk are not only leading and manipulative but loaded insofar as they impose a presupposition or assumption.

*"Why do you think the various media elite are predominantly Jewish?"[14]

*"Should our system of law and justice be based on the Christian view of man or on the humanist view of man?"[15]

"Do you agree with the author that we're in the midst of a great struggle to determine the values that will guide society?"[16]

*"Why do you think Christians and Christianity are ridiculed, demeaned, and negatively stereotyped on television?"[17]

*"Why do you think the networks include so little about Christianity in their news?"[18]

*"Why do the networks listen to and react positively to the concerns of some groups, such as homosexuals, but not Christians?"[19]

*"Why are the values undergirding the media and those undergirding the general population often so different?"[20]

"Do you agree with the author that the very foundation of Western civilization, the Christian view of man as a basis for government, is under serious attack?"[21]

Wildmon does often attempt to provide adequate evidence in support of his views, including the presuppositions of the loaded questions above. At times, the information he provides is impressive, but most of his positions are arbitrary and dogmatic, partly because the issues he has raised are more complex than he makes them appear.

The nature of our investigation does not permit us to consider in much detail the weaknesses in Wildmon's account of what he takes to be the most important form of competition between sound religion and television. However, it is useful for us to reflect on some of the stranger, or at least more contentious, of his main views. First we must take note of a whole series of problems that arise with respect to Wildmon's basic and oft-repeated claim that the "Christian view of man" traditionally was and ought to remain the "foundation" of American society. This thesis troubles me for several reasons.

1. Most students of American history, and of the history of religious liberty, know that few people have done more than the founders of the American political system to promote genuine religious liberty through some kind of separation of church and state.[22] Indeed, by the late nineteenth century, the eminent British political theorist James Bryce was moved to observe that America's institutionalized religious liberty is the salient characteristic of American culture and the one that most fundamentally distinguishes American culture from the culture of the "old world."[23] Religious liberty is a complex notion,[24] and the separation principle itself is not entirely satisfactory.[25] Nevertheless, there is probably nothing less American in spirit than the doctrine that the foundation of a society's political culture ought to be the worldview of a particular religious group. I follow those philosophers, theologians, historians, and social scientists who have argued at length that the impressive efforts of people like Roger Williams, Thomas Jefferson, and James Madison to defend religious pluralism in the United States have generally been salutary.[26]

2. A difficult question arises as to whether, or at least in what sense, the majority of Americans are or have ever been Christians. Wildmon assumes that the overwhelming majority of people in his society are

committed to some "Christian view of man," and accordingly, this view ought to be the dominant view reflected and promoted in his society's television programming. However, while recognizing that most people in their society are nominally Christian and identify themselves as Christians, other writers have suggested that, in fact, there are very few genuine Christians in any society. You may recall in this regard Donald Porter's remark that a problem posed by television to Christians is that it "normally reflects the tastes, standards and interests of the majority ... [but] the majority of people aren't Christians."[27] Wildmon himself is almost surely aware that most of the people in his society that identify themselves as Christians do not share his particular views on, say, social policy with respect to abortion, so we are left to wonder what he would make of their supposed commitment to the "Christian view of man." Indeed, a significant number of people who share Wildmon's views on subjects like abortion do not regard themselves as Christians, and would be puzzled by the suggestion that their thinking on such subjects is rooted in a specifically Christian view of man.

3. Though apparently properly trained for the ministry, Wildmon seems to be either rather naive or rather dogmatic with respect to matters of church history and theology. Wildmon knows that there are numerous Protestant denominations as well as Roman Catholic and Orthodox Christians and even some Christians who profess to be nondenominational, and that these various groups, many of which are in a sense well represented in the United States, disagree strongly on certain theological, philosophical, ethical, socio-political, and anthropological issues. Of course, professed Christians do agree on certain matters, and it is perhaps in virtue of such agreement that they are to be regarded as Christians (although again, some would argue that some of these people are not genuine Christians). But the disagreements among the various churches, denominations, and subdenominational groups in America and elsewhere would never be taken lightly by any serious student of theology or the history of religion, and such a person might well observe that the "view of man" differs significantly from one Christian group to the next. Wildmon's view of man, is, to be sure, in certain ways remarkably different from that of those who identify themselves as liberal Christians,[28] and while Wildmon may not think much of liberal Christianity, he and other Christians would do well to remember these observations of Christian scholar James Barr: "We do not have to be liberals: but we have to recognize that the liberal quest is in principle a fully legitimate form of Christian obedience within the church, and one that has deep roots within the older Christian theological tradition and even within the Bible itself."[29] Indeed, I would think that as a student of, promoter of, and spokesman for the Christian view of man, Wildmon's credentials are rather less impressive than those of, for example, Albrecht Ritschl,

Friedrich Schleiermacher, Adolf von Harnack, Shailer Matthews, Harry Emerson Fosdick, Lyman Abbott, Paul Tillich, and Hans Küng.

4. Even if we were to grant, for the sake of argument, that there has been, and in a sense still is, a precise Christian view of man shared by the overwhelming majority of Americans, the question would still arise as to why television programming should generally accommodate this perspective. Surely Wildmon and his cohorts cannot believe that if even a nominal Christianity were in fact only the faith of a tiny minority—as Christianity has often been in periods of its most sublime spiritual development, and in fact still is in most countries of the world—it would be any less worthy of promotion. They cannot be such radical conventionalists as to hold that what most people believe should ultimately count for more than what is true and good. One of the most appealing features of Biblical teaching even to those hostile to Christianity is its emphasis on doing what is right even when being mocked and persecuted by the ignorant and corrupt multitude. This is not to say that venal, self-serving elites should feel free to deceive those that they are pledged to serve; but a servile willingness to accommodate one's ideas, behavior, work, and teaching to popular attitudes and tastes is the mark of a morally deficient individual. We noted in Chapter 1 that many religious media critics believe that television programmers, goaded by advertisers and preoccupied with ratings, already cater too much to the general public's taste for the frivolous, sensationalistic, prurient, and escapist. It is not intuitively obvious that the television programmer is any more morally obliged than the Christian martyr is to accommodate popular judgments and a conventional worldview. The real issue here then is what view of man is sound, not what view of man is traditional or conventional. Wildmon's view of man may be, on balance, sounder than that of the secular humanists he denounces, but if it is, it is not so simply because many or most people in his society share it. To be sure, those responsible for television programming should not manipulate the basic beliefs and values of their audience for self-serving purposes, and they should not take lightly their influence on the judgment of viewers. But it is hard to understand why their programming should reflect any particular view of man at all, Christian or otherwise. If they do promote specific beliefs and values, they should do so for a better reason than that those are the beliefs and values that most people already hold.

5. It is important to remember that when mature people make fundamental metaphysical, moral, aesthetic, and empirical judgments, they have not just mechanically derived them from a fixed worldview that has been transmitted to them by parents, teachers, pastors, or television programmers. Although we should be careful not to underestimate the power of certain types of indoctrination and conditioning, neither should we assume that the typical individual in an advanced society is insuffi-

ciently intelligent, reflective, strong-willed, and independent to be capable of rational deliberation, imaginative insight, and existential commitment, and of distinguishing between moral principles as such and religious and ideological dogmas. One has an extremely severe and unrealistic view of man if one believes that even in advanced societies—societies having politically institutionalized freedoms of thought, conscience, religion, speech, assembly, and the press—a typical individual's personality and judgments are primarily determined by external forces that impose one of two alternative worldviews or views of man. Genuine education, of course, involves more than simply putting forward a worldview for adoption; it involves enabling people to think clearly, by and for themselves, and to do so on the basis of exposure to a wide range of ideas. Though Wildmon and other media critics are right when they say that television does not educate people as well as it could or should, television's failure in this regard should not be traced to the refusal or inability of television programmers to promote a particular view of man.

We may turn now to another basic theme of Wildmon's account, the conspiracy theory according to which there is "an intentional effort among many of the leaders of our media" to promote "the humanist view of man." This aspect of Wildmon's account also bothers me for several reasons.

1. We should first note some important ambiguities in this thesis. What kind of leaders and roughly how many of them does the author have in mind? He obviously has in mind certain television executives. It is not clear, however, how high up in the organizational hierarchy these executives have to be in order for them to qualify as leaders, nor is it clear whether Wildmon is prepared to count as leaders executives of independent companies that supply programs to the networks, producers, directors, writers, prominent news readers and reporters, hosts of widely watched talk and information shows, high-ranking executives of powerful business corporations who provide or withhold advertising revenue, major educational and legal consultants, officers of certain labor unions, and so forth. The ambiguity is crucial. For if one studies this list, one realizes that Wildmon draws the line rather arbitrarily, for, in fact, power and influence in the television industry are rather diffuse. Just as members of the same church cannot agree on certain fundamental theological and ethical issues, it hardly seems likely that all of these people in different sectors of the television industry would agree on what is the proper view of man, and on the necessity or desirability of surreptitiously foisting some such view, "humanist" or otherwise, on a mass of manipulable innocents.

Moreover, if the conception of a Christian view of man is vague and varies significantly from one Christian thinker to the next, the conception of a humanist view of man is even vaguer and even less likely to be a matter of consensus even among professed secular humanists. For one thing, I suspect that most of the people that Wildmon characterizes as secular humanists do not think of themselves as such, could not give a very satisfactory explanation of what the label signifies, and are going through life with the belief that they are "sort of religious, more or less." As for professed secular humanists, these people tend to be too independent in their thinking to go along with the authoritarianism and consensus required by maintenance of a cabal. As for Wildmon's characterization of secular humanism as a worldview or view of man promoting such things as permissiveness toward pornography,[30] drug and alcohol use,[31] sexual promiscuity,[32] and homosexual marriage,[33] most genuine secular humanists would probably in time simply be astounded by its outright absurdity.

2. Although he is none too clear on this matter, Wildmon seems to believe that the limited amount of Christian content in American television programming is in itself evidence that certain people in high places in the television industry are endeavoring to promote secular humanism. This position is a curious one on several levels. First, the question arises as to how limited the Christian content actually is, and, of course, whatever answer one gives will involve a value judgment. (A Christian fanatic could well believe that any non-Christian programming is too much.) Wildmon apparently believes that the influence of those people on network television who demean the Christian faith is greater than that of the people on network television who say positive things about and otherwise enhance the dignity of the Christian faith. Influence can be hard to measure, but it is certainly not true that there are more people on the networks demeaning the Christian faith than saying positive things about it. Blasphemers, antireligious bigots, and even serious critics of Christianity get little airtime on American network television in comparison with religious functionaries, evangelists, and show business personalities and professional athletes professing to have been "born again" or otherwise led back to Jesus. Far more characters on American television dramas and comedies are portrayed as contented participants in Christian rituals than as frustrated Christians or contented atheists. Moreover, non-Christians, humanist or otherwise, may well feel inundated by Christian symbolism, ritual, prayer, and sermonizing when they turn on their television sets at Christmas and at Easter, and even on an ordinary Sunday morning.

There is also a considerable amount of Christian and pro-Christian programming content on independent television stations and on the local affiliates of the networks. Even if this material consistently drew extremely small audiences, and this has not been the case, it could not fairly be said that the material has not been made available. At times, televangelists and other Christian preachers seem ubiquitous on the tube, and the names of many of them—Jerry Falwell, Jimmy Swaggart, Oral Roberts, and so forth—are familiar even to people who have never seen or heard them or have no interest in their message. But of far greater importance is the fact that the basic values and attitudes that animate television programming in Western societies are largely derived from Christianity, whose impact on the formation of Western culture has, after all, been unparalleled, and whose staying power, despite Wildmon's lack of faith in it, is assured in part by its historical association with Western ideals.[34]

However, even if we were to allow that the Christian and pro-Christian content in American television programming is significantly limited, we would be wise not to jump to the conclusion that this fact in itself constitutes decisive evidence that some media elite is attempting to promote a rival worldview. There could be several plausible explanations, none of which requires paranoid accusation. The first would be simply that those primarily responsible for television programming on the American networks endeavor to give the viewing audience what it wants. On one hand, such a policy is consistent with the financial concerns of television's business executives, who are almost always interested in maximizing profits, and who are ever conscious of their need to serve up those large audiences to the advertisers who provide their company with the major part of its revenue. We noted earlier that both religious and secular media critics routinely attack television for its commercialism, and Wildmon himself has sometimes joined their chorus.[35] But if a television executive is primarily concerned with maximizing the company's profits, then the matter of promoting a particular view of man is secondary at most. Even if the executive believes that promoting a more materialistic worldview will be financially useful in the long run, he or she will still be prepared to promote Christian and pro-Christian program content if it will enhance the "bottom line." But ratings and market research generally do not indicate that most viewers would rather watch programs about Jesus than detective stories and situation comedies. Thus, if programs about Jesus are less frequently scheduled than the religious media critic would like, the "blame" falls largely upon the viewers themselves, who decline to tune in to such programs. (If leaders of the television industry generally were interested more in promoting an ideology than in increasing their company's revenue, that would be reflected in their willingness to make sacrifices that, in fact, are rarely made.)

In any event, even if Wildmon is right in believing that the "values undergirding the media" are very different from those "undergirding the general population,"[36] the fact remains that, as Schultze[37] and others have observed, Christians generally choose to watch most of the same television programs that non-Christians do, and would thus appear to be rather less convinced than Wildmon and his cohorts are that such programs are demeaning them and their faith and manipulating their minds. On the other hand, television executives could have nonfinancial motives for offering the general public what they believe the public wants. And it is also important to remember that insofar as the leaders of the television industry are consciously endeavoring to limit the amount of Christian content in their programming, they may be doing so in part for reasons that have little or nothing to do with profits or ideology. They may, for example, be responding to the admonitions of high-minded critics who have declared that whenever the television industry even sincerely promotes pro-Christian program content, it necessarily bungles the job, for the nature of television as a form of technology and a medium of communication is such that it cannot do justice to the complexity of Christian spirituality.[38] Again, in determining how to manage the matter of religious program content, the broadcast industries are guided to some extent by the dictates of politicians and bureaucrats, who occasionally issue directives in this area, and who in a democratic society must respond in meaningful ways to the pressures of interest groups and the electorate itself.

3. I am inclined to agree with Wildmon and all those critics and defenders of the American television industry who see those responsible for television programming as generally being committed to certain "liberal" values and the promotion of those values. (I am not convinced that most of these people are genuine liberals, only that they are positively inclined toward particular liberal values.) Had Wildmon concentrated his attack on their liberalism rather than on their humanism, his account of competition between traditional religion and television might have been more credible. Humanism is a more attractive target for Wildmon because in its secular form it can easily be conceived as an ideology that conflicts with Christianity. Liberalism, however, is harder for people to conceive as a full-blown worldview or view of man; many Christians characterize themselves as liberals, and many liberals characterize themselves as Christians, and liberalism is widely associated exclusively with socio-political ideals. In any case, we must resist efforts to blur the conceptual distinctions between liberalism and humanism, secular or otherwise, especially when we realize that conservatives and reactionaries of all faiths have capitalized, often dishonestly, on the inability of less educated people to distinguish between the two. Unfortunately, often professed liberals and defenders of liberalism are none too clear about what being a liberal essentially involves. In fact, *liberal* and *liberalism* are extremely ambiguous terms, even if not so much so that their primary meaning cannot be distinguished from that of *secular humanism*.

When one studies the history of ordinary usage of the terms, one realizes that liberalism is primarily concerned with commitment to the values of freedom and liberty; secondarily with such more specific values as freedom of inquiry, religious freedom, religious liberty, political freedom, tolerance, individualism, and open-mindedness; and in particular contexts with economic freedom, respect for privacy, egalitarianism, belief in the moral unity of the human species, belief in the corrigibility and improvability of social and political institutions, reasonableness and rationality, scientific method, civil and political rights, resistance to arbitrary exercise of authority, the secularization of certain aspects of public life, democratic principles, emancipation from dogma and superstition, and concern for the amelioration of the condition of the underprivileged.[39] There are many things on these lists of which political and ecclesiastical conservatives, reactionaries, and radicals quite vehemently disapprove. These critics, along with some political and ecclesiastical "moderates," have often revealed significant weaknesses in certain liberal agendas. But liberalism, in any case, has no essential connection with secular humanism, atheism, or materialism; nor does it have any direct connection with the promotion of pornography, drug use, or homosexual marriage, except insofar as it advocates that individuals should, all other things being equal, be as free as possible.

Wildmon and his cohorts tend to be antagonistic to political and theological forms and aspects of liberalism, which is their privilege in a free society, but they are not intellectually sophisticated when they treat the promotion of such forms and aspects of liberalism as an attack on the Christian worldview. (As do many representatives of the "religious right" in America, Wildmon associates the antagonism of political liberals toward conservative icons like Ronald Reagan with the "humanist" contempt for the Christian view of man.[40]) There are undoubtedly many people in the television industry who are committed by deep conviction to certain traditional liberal values. Nevertheless, for people in the business of broadcasting or communications, the reinforcement of certain liberal values, in particular those associated with such civil liberties as freedom of speech and freedom of the press, is "almost an instrumental necessity," insofar as their jobs and lives are easier if they do not have to answer to external authorities.[41] This is not to say that it is always appropriate for people in the television industry to promote liberal values in the way that they do, but it is to distance their motives from those of the genuine antireligious or anti-Christian ideologist. Of course, in working to increase their autonomy and social influence at the expense of the influence of widely accepted religious authorities, they are involved in a competition with those authorities that will understandably be construed by some religionists as subversive. But what is involved here is not an intentional effort to destroy the traditional metaphysical and moral foundations of Western culture. Moreover, in setting them-

selves up, even indirectly, as inimical to the core liberal values of freedom and liberty, Wildmon and his cohorts are not doing much to
enhance their stature as good Americans and good Christians.

Having considered the two main themes of Wildmon's account, we
may consider four of the more revealing ancillary themes.

1. The claim that television tries to manipulate viewers[42] is clearly in
need of clarification and elaboration, partly because of the ambiguity of
the term *television*. Whether as a form of technology or an appliance,
television as such tries nothing; it is the people who make use of the
technology and the appliance who have aims and objectives. When one
considers the wide range of motives that lie behind intentional human
activity, one realizes that there are any number of reasons why an individual would manipulate the judgment and behavior of his fellow human beings. Manipulativeness is undoubtedly one of the regular
strategies that human beings employ in order to accomplish both narrow, personal ends and socially propitious ones. Even when manipulation has positive consequences for all parties, manipulativeness is not
entirely acceptable. Its long-term consequences cannot satisfactorily be
determined, and they may turn out to be more serious than they immediately appear to the manipulator. Manipulativeness results in cultural products that are essentially phony or inauthentic, and inasmuch
as it involves treating people as means rather than ends it requires ab-
dicating the moral point of view. So even if it yields certain positive
consequences in particular situations, it is unwholesome on a more basic
level as it is inconsistent with the respect for persons that is a primary
condition of civilization. The moral agent always avoids it where possible, preferring instead rational persuasion, education, and other approaches that involve an appeal to the higher faculties of one's fellows
and enable them to participate more fully in self-realization.

Many of those responsible for television programming do in fact routinely attempt to manipulate viewers, and I agree with critics of
commercial television programming that people in the television industry should work harder to appeal to the rational faculties and nobler
emotions of their audiences. But television programmers have not cor-
nered the market on manipulativeness. As people grow up they are often
exposed to the manipulativeness of parents, teachers, friends, colleagues,
and, to be sure, clergymen. The manipulativeness of religious functionaries is evident to anyone who has reflected on the social history of world
religions, and particularly on the institutionalized deception involved in
the principal forms of religious proselytizing.[43] Manipulativeness in television programming is no more conspicuous than in certain maneuvers
of the most prominent televangelists. And although some students of the
mass media attribute the manipulative behavior of television preachers
to their having "mimicked the methods of television,"[44] that behavior is

the application of techniques used by preachers long before the advent of television. Razelle Frankl has usefully observed that, "The history of the electric church and the use of mass communications to preach the gospel can be traced to modern revivalism as developed in the nineteenth century."[45] Actually, manipulativeness can be traced back to ancient times, when in combination with religious fervor it produced evils that Wildmon and his cohorts habitually ignore. On the other hand, serious problems may arise in assessing the appropriateness of distinguishing between manipulation and genuine education. When education of their children or fellows yields results that they find undesirable, many people are quick to jump to the conclusion that the educators in question have resorted to some devious propaganda or mind control. In fact, parents who take their young children to their own church and indoctrinate them at home with the faith of their ancestors are rather more open to the charge of being manipulative than are educators who at least later offer those children options and alternatives, expose them to a wide range of cultural and transcultural source material, and enable them to develop the cognitive and intellectual faculties conducive to independent rational judgment. If parents and religious ministers, who can have an unparalleled influence on a person's development—particularly in the formative years of childhood—are unable to compete successfully with television programming in this regard, the fault may lie more with them than with the television industry.

2. Wildmon suggests that his society is a much worse society than the American society of the 1950s, that it is overall less safe, less moral, less stable, and less just, and he identifies the mass media wolf as the principal culprit.[46] (Many people are by temperament inclined to believe that "everything is getting worse" and that we should all return to the ways of the "good old days;" preachers are often inclined to espouse this view.) I confess that on alternate days I am inclined to concur with Wildmon's assessment, but we should not ignore the ways in which the Western societies have become more civilized since the advent of television, as for example in the area of race relations (where, alas, they still have a long road to travel). Henry J. Perkinson writes that, "We continually hear much about the 'bad' effects of television and little or nothing about its 'good' effects,"[47] but television regularly "makes people more morally sensitive to their culture—more conscious of the evils it contains, or causes. And when this criticism leads, as it has, to the removal or reduction of these evils, the culture gets better."[48] It is particularly noteworthy here that to the extent that it has exposed the weaknesses and failures of institutionalized religion, and especially the corruption and hypocrisy of certain traditional religious "authorities," television programming, while on one level being in competition with traditional re-

ligion, has contributed to the melioration of institutionalized religious life in its purer and more spiritual forms.

3. Like Wildmon, I would like to see the networks include more about Christianity in their news, and I would like to see more about faiths other than Christianity. However, it is useful to consider the following observations of Judith M. Buddenbaum based on her social-scientific research: "Network newscasts devote more attention to religion than critics imagine. Between 6 and 11 percent of all stories on each of the networks during the three years covered in this study mentioned religion. Religion news stories showed up in at least half of the newscasts."[49] But Buddenbaum also found that, "Fewer than one-fifth of the religion stories focused on religion. The rest mentioned religion as a minor element in an essentially secular context,"[50] and that, "Some stories in all years gave a feel for the power and importance religious people found in faith, but at least an equal number delegitimized religion and religiously inspired concerns and behavior."[51] Buddenbaum's conclusions confirm my own suspicions with respect to this matter. Of course, none of this indicates that there is a conspiracy of a media elite to promote secular humanism, and I have indicated several reasons why concentrated television coverage of religious matters is rarer than it could be. But one of many features of Buddenbaum's analysis that interests me is its recognition that television news programming deals with religious matters in indirect as well as direct ways, and in dealing with religious matters indirectly it relates to their secular context. What Buddenbaum says of news programming applies to some extent to television programming in general. In the same volume of essays, Schultze, while acknowledging that the sharp distinction that media scholars have drawn between religious and secular programming can be valuable, adds that, "From a broader perspective, however, it is not so clear that only ostensibly religious broadcasts are religious. Only if we restrict 'religion' to the beliefs and practices of the institutional church can we legitimately claim that most television drama is not religious."[52] As in real life people do not always neatly separate the religious aspects of their worldview from the others, or divorce religious concerns and attitudes from moral, prudential, intellectual, and aesthetic concerns, so, too, television programming regularly blends the sacred with the profane.

4. We will conclude our consideration of Wildmon's perspective with some reflections on his interest in the "predominantly Jewish" presence in the "media elite." The high percentage of Jews in positions of great cultural influence—in the universities, the arts and sciences, medical research and education, the mass media, and, of course, in religious life—has over the centuries been noted with interest at many times by all sorts of cultural observers, from outright anti-Semites and philo-Semites to people with more obscure motives and interests. In the post-Holocaust

world, the more high-minded among Christian ministers habitually approach the subject rather gingerly. Mindful of the church's generally reprehensible treatment of the Jews, they are disinclined to cast any more aspersions on Jews even indirectly. Wildmon's loose talk about Jewish influence in the mass media can only trouble or offend them, and while Wildmon endeavors at times to distance himself from those who would appeal to the anti-Semitic bent of the ignorant rabble, his critics are not always impressed. Thus, Robert S. Alley writes, "Wildmon, who frequently exposes his anti-Jewish bias, does employ the buzz phrase 'Judeo-Christian heritage,' but it is always clear that by using it Wildmon sought only to counter his critics while, in fact, asserting that Jewish ethics and values were only valid when filtered through belief in Jesus as God. Wildmon unquestionably believes television is not anti-Jewish, only anti-Christian."[53] The disproportionately large presence of Jews in the television industry, particularly in the United States, is an interesting phenomenon that merits serious sociological and philosophical investigation. Indeed, the historical importance of Jews in world civilization, and in Western culture in particular, is a subject deserving of more attention than it receives from scholars in the field of cultural theory. For the time being, in any case, it will remain one of many aspects of "the mystery of the Jews" that has fascinated so many people in so many ways. The extent of "Jewish influence" in the American television industry is difficult to measure. Wildmon appears to rely heavily for his data on the Lichter and Rothman studies,[54] but many researchers have raised questions about the reliability of these studies; so that James B. Lemert observes that, "Critics of Lichter et. al. have noted that they don't share enough information about their research methodology to allow other researchers to challenge their findings by trying to replicate them."[55] In any case, the Lichters and Rothman have themselves concluded with respect to their research on the composition of the media elite that, "None of this proves that media coverage is biased. The whole notion of bias has become a straw man that obscures the far less obvious (and less nefarious) processes that mediate between journalists' perspectives and their product."[56] And Les Brown, whose criticism of the television industry is generally rather censorious, writes, "As to the idea that the networks are Eastern, liberal, and Jewish, it is largely myth."[57] Not only are there many Gentiles in high places in the industry, but the most powerful Jewish executives in the industry "move in the high social circles normally thought of as Anglo-Saxon Protestant."[58] I cannot even guess at what connection there could possibly be between the "Jewish view of man" and what Wildmon designates as the "humanist view of man," but I can state without qualification that Jewish and pro-Jewish content on American television programming is disproportionately low. Indeed, even leading Evangelical Protestant preachers have complained with respect to one of the greatest concerns of American Jews that broadcast journalists routinely exhibit a bias against the State of Israel.

But Wildmon's interest in "Jewish influence" is interesting on several levels. For one thing, despite the impressive work done in recent years by theologians, ecclesiastics, and others to promote ecumenism and interreligious dialogue—work done partly for prudential reasons, such as to improve the appearance of the churches and to create a united front against the forces of materialist secularism—Wildmon cannot conceive of the key cultural problem here as the problem of competition between television and religion. He sees it as essentially the problem of competition between television and *his* religion. And his religion is not merely the "Judeo-Christian heritage" or even Christianity as such, but his own peculiar version of Christianity, one which in certain of its fundamentals may be as far from Roman Catholicism, liberal Protestantism, and even mainstream Protestantism as it is from orthodox Judaism (which, by the way, shares Wildmon's abhorrence of such things as pornography, abortion on demand, and homosexual marriage). Thus, by his parochialism and *ressentiment*, Wildmon in effect disrupts the solidarity of the forces of religion needed for an effective competition with the forces of television, and he reduces what is a profound cultural rivalry to the status of a petty power struggle that in the end makes the socially challenging aspects of religious commitment appear much sillier and more maleficent than they already are. And curiously, Wildmon unintentionally suggests that Jewish culture is in important ways vastly superior to Christian culture, for it consistently produces a disproportionately large number of cultural leaders even despite the abusive discrimination Jews suffer at the hands of resentful Christian louts. Only when communities like the evangelical Christian congregations of Tupelo, Mississippi, start producing with more regularity great scientists, writers, intellectuals, healers, and communicators—or perhaps even a Savior—will educated and open-minded individuals be prepared to take seriously Wildmon's claim that people like him are more trustworthy "stewards" of the spiritual foundations of American culture than those clever Jews who rub him the wrong way.

Despite the numerous and serious inadequacies of his account, Wildmon is at least right to recognize that there is a crucial competition in contemporary Western societies between religion and television. Unfortunately, the importance of the competition is obscured by accounts of it that are sensationalistic and intellectually and morally careless. These accounts receive the most attention from the general public, at least in part because they suit the preference of certain leaders of the mass media for criticism that is sensationalistic, and thus easily parried. Still, in some ways we can learn as much from bad theories—once we understand why they are bad—as we can from good ones.

In examining Wildmon's conception of the primary competition between religion and television, we have taken note of a wide range of errors. When we consider these errors from the standpoint of logic and epistemology, we find that they fit certain standard patterns. There are, of course, empirical errors, errors regarding ostensibly factual claims and the evidence presented in their support. Such errors are to be challenged either by bringing forward counterexamples or more reliable testimony and research data or by showing that the limited evidence that has been adduced thus far is entirely consistent with positions other than that being advanced. These empirical errors are not always the most obvious, as determinations of what qualifies as adequate evidence can be highly subjective, and at times even as subjective as the determinations that enter into value judgments. There are also inconsistencies or contradictions, where the author is simultaneously committed to two positions that cannot reasonably be held at the same time. Then there are errors in inference, where while the premises of the author's argument are at least plausible, his conclusion does not follow from his premises. There are the usual "informal" fallacies, such as *argumentum ad hominem, argumentum ad ignorantiam, argumentum ad populum*, the fallacy of composition, hasty generalization, and the fallacy of *post hoc ergo propter hoc*. Wildmon's account is particularly rich in these. And last but not least, there are crucial ambiguities in key terms and concepts. It is necessary, of course, when we work toward developing a sound account of competition between religion and television, that we avoid as much as possible all such logical and epistemological errors. The conclusions which we will then arrive at are less likely to be as simple, straightforward, or sensational as Wildmon's, but they will be more reasonable and ultimately more instructive.

Moving on from these methodological generalities, let us consider first the human competitors involved in competition between religion and television. The people that I have reluctantly designated by such large umbrella expressions as "television programmers" and "people largely responsible for television programming" are, in fact, people with many different kinds of personal and professional backgrounds, and each of them has many different interests and aspirations, only some of which he or she shares with colleagues in the television industry. To assume that the chief financial officer of a major commercial network has the same worldview or the same basic values and concerns as the typical writer of news documentaries is to get one's analysis off on the wrong foot. To assume even that two industry executives or two writers of documentaries have precisely the same ideological attitudes and objectives is to be rather naive. And to assume that the power of the "media elite" resides almost exclusively in the hands of the business executives, or the writers, or the business executives *and* the writers, is to ignore or undervalue the potentially significant influence of news reporters, major educational and legal consultants, and others. In short, when we consider the individuals who represent the forces of television in the competition between television and religion, we see that the potential for a genuine ideological consensus, much less conspiracy, among this group of people is minimal. In the last section of this chapter, an opportunity will be given to producers, who are obviously very important in the television production and programming processes, to speak for themselves. What they have to say may be quite illuminating.

When we consider the religionists involved in the competition, we find that a parallel problem arises. The forces of religion may be seen as including all who regard themselves as religious in any sense, or only those widely regarded as being religious, or only people who profess commitment to a "Judeo-Christian heritage,"[59] or Jews and Christians, or only Christians, or only "traditional" Christians, or only conservative Christians, or only Christians with a particular type of theology, or only widely recognized religious authorities (including the authors of texts widely regarded as sacred), or only those people that the particular media critic or scholar regards as religious. When the critic or scholar makes the bold declaration that television programming tends to be antireligious or anti-Christian or inimical to traditional Christianity, we need to pay close attention to the clarity, consistency, and sensitivity to the ordinary use of language being brought to the account. But the competition that exists among religionists themselves, both in its interdenominational and intradenominational forms, is notorious. Religionists even in the same small church may routinely disagree on questions of authority, theology, and morality.

We also need to pay attention to the complexity of motives that enter into the behavior of various television people and religionists. Here we need to recognize the wide range of objects that might figure in competition between religion and television. In addition, we need to recognize that in any given situation, the individual involved in such competition may have numerous motives, even if one is primary and the others are subsidiary.[60] Furthermore, we need to remember that the objects for which people compete can be viewed at different levels of generality and specificity, so that an individual can, for example, be simultaneously seeking power, a certain kind of power, a certain kind of power over a particular group of people, and so forth.[61] A person involved in the development of television programming may be concerned with becoming wealthy and famous, while at the same time being concerned with promoting his personal worldview. But he may or may not be more concerned with the wealth and fame than with the ideological manipulation or education, and he may or may not believe that promoting his worldview will be contributive to his wealth and fame.

(Again, the words of producers in the last section of this chapter should enhance our appreciation of the complexity of at least some of the flesh-and-blood human beings involved in television production and programming.) As for religious competition, it routinely involves a wide range of objects or ends, such as economic prosperity, honor and prestige, self-respect, power and influence, God's love and affection, and salvation of one or another kind.[62]

Moreover, we must not forget that in different cases of competition between religion and television, a different group of representatives of religion and/or television may be involved, or the same group of representatives may be focusing on objectives that do not concern it in other cases. So, for example, in a particular situation, it may be writers and creative artists alone who represent the competitors with the forces of religion, and it may be the ecclesiastical elites alone who represent the competitors with the forces of television. In another situation, television executives may be more concerned than usual with educational objectives—for even the most venal television executive does occasionally stand up for his or her pet moral cause—and religious reformers may be more concerned than usual with their personal glory—as even the most saintly individuals are occasionally concerned about their public image and how they will be judged by posterity.

What we have learned from our critique of Wildmon's account should also prod us to consider the complexity of competition itself. First, what degree of awareness does a particular competition involve? Are people usurpers if they are not aware of the effects of their activity? Can there be competition which, though not open, does not qualify as surreptitious or conspiratorial? Can there be genuine competition involving only one striver?[63] Second, we must consider what the explicit or implicit rules are that are relevant to the ascription of fairness and unfairness in a particular competition. Is a particular competition necessarily unfair when one or more competitors refuses or fails to reveal his specific aims and objectives? Can a competition be fair or unfair if the various competitors are not even aware of general rules that ought to govern competition, or do not believe that such rules exist, or cannot agree on what the rules ought to be?[64] With respect to competition between religion and television, when if ever is manipulation an acceptable substitution for rational persuasion and education? And how much pressure can fairly be put on governmental and other external agencies to establish regulations that will alter the balance of power between the interests of the television industry and those of major religious hierarchies? Third, it helps to have reasonably assessed the value of both competition as such and the particular competition under consideration. Do the advantages of the competitive spirit outweigh its disadvantages? More specifically, should the satisfaction that successfully competing gives an individual or group be regarded as counting for more than the animosity that vigorous competition can engender? Or again, should the choice that competition provides consumers or clients be seen as counting for more than the disruption that such competition may cause to the philosophical unity of the community in question?[65] One's assessment of a particular competition involves any number of subjective factors, and of course, philosophers and social scientists have long disagreed concerning whether competition as such is salutary for individuals and communities—and concerning what degree and kinds of competition are salutary for individuals and communities.

Additional questions arise as to how much competitors may reasonably be expected to compete for the sake of others—both in specific groups that they are pledged to serve and in the society as a whole—in addition to competing for their own private concerns. In assessing competition, serious inquirers must consider the competition in relation to the highest trans-cultural ideals, which in fact themselves regularly enter into a kind of competition. It is no easy task for the moralist to determine the appropriate balance in a given situation between considerations of freedom and justice, freedom and happiness, truth and happiness, justice and happiness, and so forth. A genuine moral agent who considers some aspect of competition between religion and television will not be content with appeals to this or that tradition or to conventional opinion, and he certainly will not promote the principle that in the end, social policy is to be determined by brute force, deception, or sophisticated public relations rather than by extensive public dialogue among those who try hard to realize such trans-cultural ideals as wisdom, justice, commitment, integrity, and compassion. I grant that what I have just said has more than a touch of the unworldly (and perhaps religious) about it, but I earnestly believe that if the majority of people in our society worked harder at being morally responsible in their personal and professional lives, and at producing and promoting authentic rather than phony cultural products, they would not only be better and happier individuals, but would have a far better chance of solving such problems as how to bring about more constructive relations between religion and television.

We have now considered a large number of factors that can make the task of providing a reliable account of even a particular competition between religion and television extremely arduous, and have considered further some of the subjective judgments that necessarily enter into any such account. We are thus safeguarded for the time being against the overgeneralization, excessive speculation, and self-righteousness that vitiate simplistic and sensationalistic analyses. But recognizing the complexity of a problem does not make the problem evaporate. The issues and concerns surveyed in Chapter 1 are serious. Responsible judgment

in any domain—scientific, moral, aesthetic, and so forth—frequently requires the weighing of many factors that are ignored or undervalued by
impatient, undisciplined agents, but we all have to make judgments. We
are better equipped to make sound ones if we appreciate relevant considerations that less conscientious people fail to take into account. Most
of the positions that we considered in Chapter 1, though somewhat
vague and speculative, are at least clear and plausible enough to inspire
in the student of contemporary culture a desire to contrive possible solutions to what may be among the most important cultural problems of
our day. And while it is useful to recognize that we must often set aside
the big questions of cultural theory and social policy and focus instead
on the details of a particular case, the big questions need to be addressed
too, and for practical reasons must be regarded as answerable in some
sense. Moreover, even if we were committed to considering only particular forms of competition between religion and television, we could not
reasonably expect our fellows to rely consistently on ad hoc devices for
balancing the interests and influences of competing cultural forces and
relieving tensions among them that clearly have persisted over time.

Religious media critics who have recognized the inadequacy of simplistic and sensationalistic accounts like Wildmon's have usually prof-
fered practical solutions to the general type of cultural problem
considered in Chapter 1. Many of their recommendations are somewhat
vague, and some verge on being platitudinous, and it is often difficult
to see how such recommendations could be put to use in dealing with
particular cases. Still, even the vaguer recommendations are of some
value, insofar as they direct our attention to the possible role of institutions such as the family and the school. Most emphasize the importance
of some form of discussion, education, activism, or pluralism. For example, Schultze recommends at one point that, "[P]arents and children
together discuss why particular shows are unacceptable or worthwhile,"[66] and Postman declares that, "The desperate answer is to rely on
the only mass medium of communication that, in theory, is capable of
addressing the problem: our schools."[67] Steve Bruce, who envisions the
fundamental problem quite differently than Schultze and Postman, argues that, "A society of fundamentalists, liberal Protestants, Catholics,
Jews, Mormons, Muslims, and atheists reduces conflict by allowing enormous variety of religious expression in private and permitting only the
blandest religion in the public arena."[68] And Michael R. Real, who con-
ceives of religion as "a major subsystem of culture and society, along
with the subsystems of economics, politics, sports and recreation, education, and the family,"[69] offers a broader and more inclusive solution
in line with his broader and more inclusive conception of the basic cultural problem:

Mass-mediated culture can be rendered more understandable and humanistic by increasing cultural studies and policy research, by continuing consumer activism and reform efforts, by reducing the role of private capital and profit, by reversing authoritarian one-way transmission, by decentralizing, and by developing in the wake of structural revolution a cultural revolution that returns to the top priority the full, collective humanity of persons, the value of life, and the appreciation and balanced development of the environment.[70]

Four more specific proposals also regularly surface. The first is that rather than focusing on the negative cultural impact of television, religionists and religious institutions should simply concentrate on working more effectively at performing their traditional religious duties. Underlying this proposal is the high-minded (and prudent) attitude that people must not become so preoccupied with the tactics and successes of their rivals that they lose sight of their own capabilities and responsibilities. But if this proposal is seen as counseling the forces of religion to resign from competition with their cultural rivals, then following it to its logical conclusion may ultimately involve giving up the good cause, for religions can only hope to fulfill the major socio-cultural objectives of their traditional agenda if they can successfully counter or neutralize the most threatening tactics of their rivals. (No matter how excellent the products they produce, the manufacturers of motorcars and soft drinks simply cannot afford to ignore what their competitors are doing. Even Jesus, while enjoining his followers to "resist not evil,"[71] expected them to do what is necessary to "teach all nations, baptizing them in the name of the Father, and of the Son, and of the Holy Ghost."[72]) If, however, the proposal is not interpreted or extended in this way, then it by implication acknowledges the necessity of dealing to some extent and in some way with the competition that television gives religion.

A second proposal is to turn the matter of balancing the cultural interests and influences of religionists and television people over to some third party, normally a government agency. Though they would probably be reluctant to admit it, people who look to the government to be the arbiter in disputes over cultural turf between religious organizations and broadcasting organizations believe that such disputes are a political concern, a matter of keeping the peace and establishing certain civil conditions of social justice. Religious organizations are more prone than broadcasting organizations to run to the government for protective arbitration and legislation; they more often feel threatened by their rival. However, broadcasters, too, have been known to seek shelter under the outstretched wing of the political establishment, as for example when threatened with boycotts, subjected to personal vilification in reactionary mass media, and generally exposed to the pressure tactics of religious interest groups. And we should not assume that government regulation tends to favor religious organizations over broadcasting organizations. For one thing, politicians, whose relations with religious leaders and groups have throughout history taken many different forms,[73] are not necessarily either sympathetic or antipathetic to religious interests. Also, in advanced Western democracies, government agencies have probably expended more effort on reining in religious groups attempting to use the airwaves than impressing upon broadcasters the cultural importance of devoting more quality airtime to promoting religious attitudes and values.

A case can be made for looking at some point to the government to reconcile the competing demands of religious organizations and broadcasting organizations. Officers of state have a distinctive form of authority, one derived at least in part from their association with civil law and order. In advanced democratic societies, politicians theoretically are elected by all the people and represent citizens of all faiths and professions. Although they are expected to respect freedoms of religion and expression, they are seen as having an authority that transcends that of the leaders of particular faith communities and media organizations within the state.[74] One dimension of their authority involves a public mandate to promote the conditions of cultural development.[75] Nevertheless, dumping this cultural problem into the laps of politicians is neither wise nor prudent, and ordinarily has the marks of a desperate measure. Whenever one side in a competition petitions government officials to establish conditions of fair competition, by its action it acknowledges its own frailty and leaves itself open to the criticism that it is a sore loser incapable of properly managing its own affairs and of demonstrating the value of its product. Again, while both religious leaders and mass media leaders have historically entered into all sorts of mutually beneficial alliances with politicians, they have generally been aware of the danger of becoming entirely dominated by politicians, who do have a professional proclivity to extend their power and influence. While religionists and workers in the mass media often turn to the state to protect their freedoms of religion and expression,[76] most of them know that throughout history the leaders of the state have periodically been the most ruthless enemies of such groups.[77] Politicians and the bureaucrats serving under them have no special insight enabling them to make astute judgments concerning the competing cultural interests and influences of religion and television. For all their interest in extending their power, most politicians in democratic societies may well prefer to avoid taking on the role of arbiter here, for they are habitually loath to risk offending constituents who already have a fairly clear conception of what kind of religion and what kind of television they like. In an undemocratic state, arbitration in disputes of this kind can take quite different forms, from the arbitrary self-assertion of a bigoted despot to the careful application of conciliatory procedures by an enlightened ruling class.

In advanced democratic societies, the competing cultural forces of religion and television may get less direction and support through political arbitration and legislation than they expect or require. Politicians in these societies are often capable of a cautiousness or evasiveness here that they do not manifest in other areas of policy-making, which is reflected in the cant that commonly marks official government documents and white papers in the area. When one considers, for example, the history of political regulation of broadcasting in Canada,[78] one may first be struck by how little attention has been given in national broadcasting acts and policy statements to the subject of religion and broadcasting, especially in contrast with the attention given to such issues as the appropriate means of establishing and reinforcing a national cultural identity and the appropriate means of providing information of use to voters. Even so, what is perhaps the most important document in the history of Canadian broadcasting policy, the 1929 report of the Aird Commission,[79] was prompted largely by a controversy involving religion and broadcasting. As Roger Bird explains:

The first of many public inquiries into broadcasting in Canada was provoked in 1928 by a mix of politics, religion, and radio. Among the radio stations operated by churches were four run by the International Bible Students Association, an organization affiliated with the Jehovah's Witnesses church. The Minister of Marine and Fisheries, P. J. Arthur Cardin, told the House of Commons that these stations had been the target of complaints about programs that were allegedly "unpatriotic and abusive of all our churches.[80]

Focusing arbitrarily on the circumstances of this particular case, the Aird Commission came up with only this remarkably arbitrary recommendation about relations between religion and broadcasting: "[T]hat where religious broadcasting is allowed, there should be regulations prohibiting statements of a controversial nature or one religion making an attack upon the leaders or doctrine of another."[81] Over the years, Canadian broadcasting regulators, while affirming the principle that the medium of broadcasting should remain "at the disposal of the nation, regardless of party, section, class or religion,"[82] have basically attempted to deal with tensions between the cultural forces of religion and broadcasting by focusing (arbitrarily) on a rather vague ideal of inclusiveness involving "equal and fair presentation of all main points of view."[83] However, it has rarely been clear to interested parties what realization of this ideal requires, or how attempts at realizing it represent the most significant possible contribution that politicians and bureaucrats can make to the kind of cultural advancement that concerns high-minded media critics, religious and otherwise. In any case, religious and media interest groups can hardly expect much better when they themselves expend so much effort endeavoring to influence the decisions of politicians and bureaucrats.

A third proposal deserving of attention is that representatives of religious groups and the mass media more vigorously pursue forms of cooperation that, while they may not end or replace competition between the two camps, will mitigate tensions, contribute to mutual understanding and appreciation, and provide incentives to further dialogue. Many religious leaders recognized from its beginnings how television could be utilized for religious purposes; as Peter G. Horsfield notes, in the United States, "[R]eligious programs were among the first year's offerings on television in 1940," and this followed a pattern whereby, "Each time a new mass medium has emerged, the church has been there and adapted the medium's use to the church's purpose."[84] Those responsible for television programming may have felt over the years some degree of pressure to cooperate with religious institutions, but this cooperation has promoted goodwill toward the industry and has both directly and indirectly been a source of revenue. Cooperation that is not pursued under compulsion will usually prove to be beneficial to both camps (although less often so to society itself), but often it will not be easy. For one thing, the agendas of religionists and television people are in some ways so different that often there will not be enough common ground on which to locate mutual advantage; that, after all, is why the relationship between the cultural forces of religion and television is so often competitive. Furthermore, religious leaders and media leaders may have trouble participating in the genuine dialogue that is a prerequisite of successful cooperation. Religious leaders are often superior communicators, but frequently they cannot break out of a pattern common to all authorities— that of finding it much harder to talk *with* people than *to* them.[85] Similarly, people in the television industry are vocationally involved in a one-way transmission often accompanied by authoritarian overtones.[86]

A fourth proposal is that religionists themselves infiltrate the television industry, or alternatively, create a rival television industry that operates under religious auspices. Although these are actually two distinct proposals, I treat them as two aspects of the same proposal because many people who advocate this sort of thing do not distinguish clearly between the two options. In both cases, emphasis is placed on transforming the television industry itself. In the first, however, the idea of what constitutes the industry is restricted to the existing institution, while in the second, the industry is conceived more abstractly in terms of possibilities. So, for example, Stephen R. Lawhead writes bluntly that, "[T]he proper Christian attitude toward popular culture should be one of attack—an aggressive infiltration of contemporary culture by informed Christian consumers and artists."[87] David Porter makes the point almost as militantly: "We need Christian journalists, Christian artists, Christian musicians, Christian poets, Christian film-makers, and Christians in television. . . . We need to bring all our fighters into the battle."[88] (Porter explicitly refers to the value of "a Christian industry to sell our message."[89]) A rather more subtle but no less assertive version of the proposal was made many years ago by a group of Christian researchers studying the broadcasting industry:

The Church should help every one of its members to translate the moral principles of Christianity into effective vocational action. The owner or manager of an industry, the worker employed in it, the legal counsel that serves it, the social workers, educators, and other public servants whose vocation compels them to concern themselves with the industry's product, with its standards of employment and its public relations—all these vocational groups include persons who are members of Christian churches. If the religion they find fostered there is vital, it will have a message relevant to their vocations.[90]

But the religious media critic is not necessarily entitled to the last word on all these matters. The representatives and defenders of television have something to contribute here, too. As it happens, once religious media critics stop blaming them for the decline of Western civilization, imputing to them all kinds of unscrupulous and concealed motives and dismissing their work as fluff, junk, or the propaganda of barbarism, the cultural forces of television will be ready to reveal that their own solutions to the concerns raised in Chapter 1 are not necessarily different from those of insecure religionists. They will contend, perhaps with no less sincerity than the cultural forces of religion, that they, too, believe in the value of discussion, education, activism, and pluralism. There is plenty of discussion on television in the North American and Western European democracies; learned experts and the common man and woman are paraded before the viewer on talk shows and information shows.

Much of the educational programming that television offers is simply taken for granted, but one can even get university credits for some of the things one learns from television; one can learn about everything from cuisine, motorcar repair, and the latest medical discoveries to the historical circumstances that have led up to the momentous political events reshaping the modern world. Whatever forms of passivity it may engender, television must be credited with having made a significant contribution to the rebelliousness of young idealists who have been far more radical and assertive than their ancestors raised in pre-television days. Thus, for example, as Steven Starker points out, "Those convinced of the pathological passivity of the television generations must have been surprised by the political activism and commitment shown by so many young people during the Vietnam War."[91] As for pluralism, what other medium of communication so inclusively provides a forum to both bishops and prostitutes, poets and terrorists, physicians and racketeers, celebrities and nobodies? It can surely do much better than it has in all of these areas, but those responsible for its programming have not placed themselves beyond criticism, and have even made a forum available to some of their most hostile critics, including Wildmon and his ilk. Furthermore, they have never discouraged families from discussing which programs are worthwhile and which are not, they have regularly sought the advice of prominent educational theorists and child psychologists, and they have raised the profile of consumer activists like Ralph Nader even at the expense of offending some of their most powerful advertisers.

Again, they have generally concerned themselves with looking after their own business, and have not spent the time that the cultural forces of religion have spent waving an accusatory finger at their "rivals," and they have usually asked little more from politicians than that they be left alone as much as possible. They have often indicated a willingness to cooperate with religious groups and have done much, if not as much as they could, to put religion and religionists in a good light. No substantial evidence has yet to appear that the television industry in any of the Western democracies has sought to undermine developing religious networks and production companies, or has systematically denied employment or equality of opportunity to devout men and women. And most importantly, television in the Western democracies has from its earliest days offered a substantial amount of religious programming and programming involving religious themes, and the variety of these kinds of programming that it has offered is customarily ignored or forgotten.

As for the inadequacies of much of this programming, these can hardly be blamed exclusively on television executives, producers, writers, and their colleagues. If television has been made available as an instrument to religious leaders and groups and has been poorly utilized by them, the fault may lie at least as much with religionists as with people in the television industry. Indeed, it may lie very much more with religionists, and perhaps with institutionalized religion itself. But then, religious television may not be nearly as bad as most of its critics would have us believe. These are matters that merit more than passing consideration.

Thus far, ample opportunity has been afforded to religious media critics and various intellectuals and observers to speak in their own voice. I have taken it upon myself to speak for television people in articulating the kind of responses that reflective representatives of this group might offer when confronted with the charge that there is something subversive in their general program with respect to its treatment of and influence upon the traditional forms of religious spirituality. Given the nature of their work and their training, people in the television crafts and industries cannot reasonably be expected to discourse as freely and comfortably about religious and philosophical subjects as religious thinkers, intellectuals, and other cultural theorists can about television—particularly, television in a broad cultural context. There are, to be sure, many very intelligent people working in television crafts and industries, and undoubtedly a significant number of them are given to reflection on religious, philosophical, moral, and cultural subjects; but mindful of their own limitations in expressing themselves clearly in these areas, as well as of the perils of offending cultural representatives of erudition and high spirituality, they generally opt to express themselves through the television crafts and productions that they know so much better. When overly bold television celebrities speak loosely about high matters that they know little about, they may impress a lot of naive and ignorant people, but they also embarrass their wiser colleagues. The brightest people in the television crafts prudently avoid such publicity. But these bright people may well have something special to contribute to discussion and understanding of the cultural relations of religion and television, particularly when they rise to speak in their own defense, or at least show us that what they are trying to accomplish is indeed culturally constructive after all.

If there is one sub-group of television people that warrants particular consideration in this study, it is the producers—particularly, working producers of television films. A widely held view among advanced students of mass communications is that television, unlike, say, theater or film, is a "producer's medium," insofar as in television the producer is the "focal point for bringing the message to the audience."[92] Alan Wurtzel and Stephen R. Acker have observed that,

One reason for the producer's central role in television is the nature of the television business. Television requires a constant source of program material, and while many people are continually involved in producing specific television programs, most team members join a show only when their talents are needed, perform their jobs, and then leave the production once their contribution is over. Only the producer, and perhaps a few members of the producer's staff, actually stay with the show from its earliest inception until its ultimate broadcast or distribution. The producer must give a sense of continuity and unity to the production, since he or she is the one person who knows how all the different parts of the show will ultimately fit together.[93]

The producer, Wurtzel and Acker suggest, must be something of a "Renaissance person"[94] who knows something about the creative, organizational, and business aspects of television programming and must be able to plan the entire operation.[95] "In television, the producer develops the program idea, supervises the entire production from the first pre-production meeting to the last videotape edit, and has the ultimate responsibility for every element—both technical and creative—that goes into the production."[96] The producer thus must know the subject,[97] and more specifically, develop a program idea, research the idea, know the particular audience, and do audience research.[98] Producers have responsibility for what is known in their craft as preparing the "program treatment" and "production book."[99] They are also responsible for budgeting work, selling the project, personnel management, copyright clearance, scheduling, and promotion.[100] Additionally, as the pure business executive, writer, and director must, the producer must respond to the demands of interest groups and government agencies.[101]

Individuals who have the talent necessary for successfully carrying out these responsibilities are not to be taken lightly. When certain high-minded critics of television programming rant about "those responsible" for such programming, we would do well to remind ourselves of the wide-ranging intelligence, skill, and personal style that competent producers must bring to their work. We should not lose sight of the fact that these talented people are indeed individuals. Academic humanists Horace Newcomb and Robert S. Alley, scholars well familiar with religious and other lofty criticism of television programmers, have stressed the importance of getting beyond the anonymity of television[102] in order to appreciate how much television is not merely a "generalized force let loose in the home and in society"[103] but something that involves individuals,[104] and more precisely, creative individuals.[105] With that point in mind, Newcomb and Alley actually went to the trouble of interviewing leading television producers, and it is noteworthy that the famous producers we meet in the Newcomb and Alley interviews are not nearly as venal, shallow, materialistic, or one-dimensional as the loudest critics of television programming would have us believe.

The television producers that Newcomb and Alley interviewed did not directly address the question of the cultural relations of religion and television, and their references to religion as such were oblique. But helped along by the sometimes generous (and occasionally leading) questions of Newcomb and Alley, they come across as bright, reasonable, imaginative, congenial, socially constructive fellows. For example, Earl Hamner, producer of *The Waltons*, a sensitive dramatic series widely acclaimed for its touching and insightful exploration of family relationships and social problems, says, "I think what motivates me is that I am basically a story-teller. I enjoy telling stories . . . especially in television."[106] (*The Waltons* was based on a television movie that was in turn based on one of Hamner's own novels.) Hamner recognizes the wide range of personality types who work in his field, and in an interestingly ambiguous comment, he remarks that, "I'm beginning to sound like a Baptist preacher, but I think that what you see on any television show reflects the morals and the conscience of the people on those shows who have influence. I have an affirmative, upright, cheerful view of humanity, and I think that that's reflected in the show."[107] The affirmative, upright, cheerful Hamner, who produced such television movies as *Heidi* and *Charlotte's Web*, might strike certain reactionary critics of American television programming as a remarkable exception to the rule, but it is noteworthy that he was also the producer of the often steamy prime-time soap opera, *Falcon Crest*.

Then there is the case of Quinn Martin, producer of such famous detective-suspense shows as *The Fugitive, Cannon, Barnaby Jones,* and *The Streets of San Francisco*. These shows might seem on the surface to have catered basically to their audience's craving for fast action, car chases, violence, and revenge. Martin does not see himself as a great moralist and admits quite frankly that his primary aim as a producer has been to entertain. But he adds, without a trace of pretence or self-consciousness: "In fifteen hundred shows I tried to have a theme, whether it be as simple as 'good conquers evil,' or 'live by the sword, die by the sword,' even 'nice guys don't have to finish last.' It doesn't have to be heavy but I do think you can have a little substance in what you're doing as long as you entertain them [audiences] along the way."[108] Is not such "substance" compatible with, or perhaps derived from, the moral and spiritual wisdom of the world's great ancient faiths?

And then, of course, there is Norman Lear, that conspicuous object of Pastor Wildmon's disapproval.[109] He told Newcomb and Alley, "It is too easy to be self-serving, talking about one's work. But I think I and the wonderful group of people with whom I collaborate are basically in love with humanity. I think we all step off of the same philosophical base, feeling people are fundamentally good."[110] Well, this philosophical base is one which many a Christian theologian will decline to step off of, but with a felicitous blend of humility and self-respect, Lear can add, "I would be a horse's ass if I thought that one little situation comedy would accomplish something that the entire Judeo-Christian ethic hasn't managed in two thousand years. But there have been some specific results, results that were measurable."[111] Detractors, take note: however shaky his philosophico-theological base may be, Lear can get socially constructive results, and measurable ones, too.

But Lear has also revealed an important limitation of the project of Newcomb and Alley. It is often easy to be self-serving when talking about one's work, especially when being interviewed by gracious fellows who are out to prove that one is more creative and less corrupt than assumed to be by reactionary critics. The questions of Newcomb and Alley do not probe in a direction that would satisfactorily reveal to us, for example, why the producer of *The Waltons* would devote so much creative time and effort to producing something like *Falcon Crest*, or why Quinn Martin would rather devote his career to turning out fifteen hundred forgettable shows than turning out three or four genuine masterpieces, or why Norman Lear has so much trouble coming to grips with the fundamental character of human evil. More importantly, the producers interviewed by Newcomb and Alley can hardly be blamed for wanting to seem as appealing as possible. These highly successful producers are by the nature of their vocation much more adept at public relations than most plain folks.

Thus, it is useful to consider here the valuable work of sociologist Muriel G. Cantor. When Cantor arrived in Los Angeles, she was favorably impressed by various television people that she met socially. Recognizing their intelligence and other personal qualities, she was led to reflect on the contrast between these real human beings and the most common stereotypes of people in their industry, as well as on the contrast between their own talent and the mediocrity and unimaginativeness of so much television programming.[112] Recognizing the working television producer's key role and relative power in the industry, a role and power directly related to the producer's executive and creative authority and responsibility,[113] she, too, went to the trouble of interviewing television producers. But unlike the producers interviewed for the Newcomb and Alley study, the producers interviewed by Cantor generally remain anonymous in her social-scientific research report.

Although the relevance of that fact should not be overestimated, it undoubtedly does go some way toward explaining notable differences between Cantor's view of television producers and the view of Newcomb and Alley. It is also important to appreciate here that Newcomb and Alley, being more humanistic in orientation, were intent upon focusing on the creativity of producers, whereas Cantor, as a social-scientific researcher, was more concerned with the limits of the producers' creative control and their modes of adaptation to the problem posed by those limits. Reflecting on the Newcomb-Alley approach, Cantor suggested that it "can be called an 'auteur' approach" because Newcomb and Alley "see television as primarily a producer's medium and, as such, producers are 'cultural carriers'." For Newcomb and Alley, Cantor observed, television producers "also bear the responsibility for the programs and the messages they give."[114] But with her sociological perspective and agenda, Cantor was less concerned with the producers' creativity as such and more concerned with the conditions under which that creativity can flourish.[115]

The Newcomb-Alley study stresses the individuality of television producers and their common creativity. In the tradition of the classical sociologists, Cantor focuses more on types, and so the differences among television producers take on a special significance. Thus, one of the anonymous producers interviewed by Cantor observed that, "One of the reasons so many shows fail is that the networks and others underestimate the IQ of the audience. . . . There should be shows with more character and originality that tap the more intelligent audience."[116] But another of the producers said bluntly that, "[We] try not to do anything controversial. Nor do we try to reach people of high intellect. Because of this we are a success."[117] Perhaps most telling is the testimony of the producer who told Cantor that, "I try to keep everybody happy without selling my soul."[118]

Cantor concluded that there are three basic types of working producers of television films: "film makers," generally younger people with formal training who are more interested in fame than money; "writers-producers," who would like to make more meaningful television films with social messages and are more interested in content than in technical aspects of production; and "old-line producers," mainly concerned with financial success and popularity.[119] Although such a typology necessarily involves a certain degree of oversimplification, it draws our attention to the fact that when considering the ambitions and aspirations of television producers—and of other people responsible for television programming—we should bear in mind that there are patterns and types in addition to individual differences and common concerns.

Cantor was particularly interested in the different modes of adaptation that different types of producers follow in order to operate in the system.[120] "All three types of producers perform the same or similar tasks. . . . Yet all three types see their occupational roles differently, and consequently each reacts differently to bureaucratic controls and bureaucratic standards."[121] Those of the film maker type tend to be "more compatible with the system" than the writers-producers,[122] as the latter come "closer to the ideal of the lone creator" and are "more similar to the artist, composer, and playwright than the other two types."[123] The old-line producers, of course, tend to "see themselves as businessmen producing entertainment as a product."[124]

The producer George Heinemann has been quoted as saying that producing is 60 percent organization and 40 percent creativity.[125] This concept of organization is a rather nebulous one. Confronted with the subject of the relation of television producers to the television programming that they are seen as producing, Cantor herself was struck by the complexity of the question of how content is chosen, and was moved to insist that the "whole social fabric must necessarily be studied" if sophisticated answers to the question are to emerge in the future.[126] All television producers are creative in a certain sense, and some are particularly creative in rather lofty and imposing ways. It is appropriate to regard all television producers as free and responsible agents in a certain general way, and to regard individual television producers as relatively free and responsible agents in various specific ways. But all television producers are to some extent creatures of the industrial system in which they operate, even if some are much more independent-minded than others. More importantly, they are all to some extent creatures of vastly more expansive systems that require proficiency at organizational work and yet to a great extent remain intractable even to the most adept organizers. One such system is the "whole social fabric" to which Cantor has referred. If we take a wider view, we may see another such system as the "natural order," the "cosmos," "reality," or the "divine creation."

Reconciling free will, personal responsibility, and creativity with such determining factors as social conditioning and indoctrination—or for that matter, instinct and genetic inheritance—is not the kind of problem that could ever be fully and satisfactorily solved. Viewed in its most abstract form, it is a metaphysical problem of reconciling free agency, responsibility, and creativity with causal determinism. Viewed in its most profound historical form, it is derived from the problem of reconciling the freedom and responsibility of mere mortals with the omnipotence and omniscience of a transcendent creative force. Religious and other media critics who are quick to cast aspersions on "those responsible" for the degraded state of television programming are often lacking in sociological, anthropological, sociobiological, philosophical, and even theological insight into the complexity of the problem of freedom versus determinism. Still, few of those that they criticize would deny that in important ways they are indeed free, responsible, and creative agents. When they speak in their own voice, most producers and others involved in the television crafts affirm this great existential faith.

Having granted that point, we may turn to the subject of religious television. What precisely is religious television, and is it nearly as bad as its most severe critics would have us believe?

NOTES TO CHAPTER 2

1. Cf. Donald E. Wildmon, *The Home Invaders* (Wheaton, IL: SP Publications, 1985), p. 5.

2. See, for example, Mary Whitehouse, *Cleaning-Up TV: From Protest to Participation* (London: Blandford Press, 1967).

3. John 10:11–15.

4. Plato *Republic* 343B.

5. Ibid., 345B–D.

6. Quentin J. Schultze, *Television: Manna from Hollywood?* (Grand Rapids, MI: Zondervan, 1986), p. 15.

7. Cf. Wildmon, *The Home Invaders*, p. 5.

8. Ibid.

9. Ibid., p. 14.

10. Ibid., p. 105.

11. Ibid., p. 130.

12. Ibid., p. 181.

13. Ibid., p. 38.

14. Ibid., p. 31.

15. Ibid., p. 43.

16. Ibid., p. 50.

17. Ibid.

18. Ibid., p. 74.

19. Ibid.

20. Ibid., p. 125.

21. Ibid., p. 182.

22. Cf. Jay Newman, *On Religious Freedom* (Ottawa: University of Ottawa Press, 1991), pp. 111–12.

23. Cf. M. Searle Bates, *Religious Liberty: An Inquiry* (New York: Da Capo Press, 1972), p. 288. This volume is a reprint of a work first published in 1945 under the auspices of the World Council of Churches.

24. Cf. Newman, *On Religious Freedom*, ch. 4.

25. Ibid., pp. 113–23.

26. Ibid., pp. 123–41.

27. Cf. David Porter, *The Media: A Christian Point of View* (London: Scripture Union, 1974), pp. 55–56.

28. Cf. Newman, *On Religious Freedom*, ch. 5.

29. James Barr, *Fundamentalism* (Philadelphia: Westminster Press, 1977), p. 344.

30. Wildmon, *The Home Invaders*, p. 29.

31. Ibid., pp. 156, 159.

32. Ibid., p. 94.

33. Ibid., pp. 125, 142, 147, 154.

34. Cf., for example, Christopher Dawson, "Religion and Life," in *Enquiries into Religion and Culture* (New York: Sheed and Ward, 1933), pp. 292–310; R. G. Collingwood, *An Essay on Metaphysics* (Oxford: Clarendon Press, 1940), ch. 21; T. S. Eliot, *Notes towards the Definition of Culture* (London: Faber and Faber, 1948), pp. 27–31, 122–23.

35. Wildmon, *The Home Invaders*, p. 90.

36. Ibid., p. 125.

37. Schultze, *Television: Manna from Hollywood?*, p. 12.

38. Cf., for example, Neil Postman, *Amusing Ourselves to Death: Public Discourse in the Age of Show Business* (New York: Viking, 1985), pp. 87, 116–21, 159; Peter G. Horsfield, *Religious Television: The American Experience* (New York: Longmans, 1984), p. 69; Quentin Schultze, *Televangelism and American Culture: The Business of Popular Religion* (Grand Rapids, MI: Baker Book House, 1991), p. 119; Stewart M. Hoover, *Mass Media Religion: The Social Sources of the Electronic Church* (Newbury Park, CA: Sage Publications, 1988), p. 237; James B. Twitchell, *Carnival Culture: The Trashing of Taste in America* (New York: Columbia University Press, 1992), p. 243.

39. Newman, *On Religious Freedom*, pp. 144–50. Cf., for example, J. Salwyn Schapiro, *Liberalism: Its Meaning and History* (Princeton, NJ: D. Van Nostrand, 1958); John Gray, *Liberalism* (Milton Keynes, England: Open University Press, 1986).

40. Cf. Wildmon, *The Home Invaders*, p. 161.

41. Cf. Herbert J. Gans, *Deciding What's News: A Study of* CBS Evening News, NBC Nightly News, Newsweek, *and* Time (New York: Pantheon Books, 1979), p. 207.

42. Wildmon, *The Home Invaders*, p. 43.

43. Cf. Jay Newman, *Foundations of Religious Tolerance* (Toronto: University of Toronto Press, 1982), ch. 5; Jay Newman, *Competition in Religious Life*, Editions SR, Vol. 11 (Waterloo, ON: Wilfrid Laurier University Press, 1989), ch. 3.

44. Stewart M. Hoover, *The Electronic Giant: A Critique of the Telecommunications Revolution from a Christian Perspective* (Elgin, IL: The Brethren Press, 1982), p. 123.

45. Razelle Frankl, *Televangelism: The Marketing of Popular Religion* (Carbondale: Southern Illinois University Press, 1987), p. 4.

46. Wildmon, *The Home Invaders*, p. 43.

47. Henry J. Perkinson, *Getting Better: Television and Moral Progress* (New Brunswick, NJ: Transaction Publishers, 1991), p. 1.

48. Ibid., p. 9.

49. Judith M. Buddenbaum, "Network News Coverage of Religion," in John P. Ferré, ed., *Channels of Belief: Religion and American Commercial Television* (Ames: Iowa State University Press, 1990), p. 76.

50. Ibid.

51. Ibid., p. 78.

52. Quentin J. Schultze, "Television Drama as a Sacred Text," in Ferré, ed., *Channels of Belief*, p. 27.

53. Robert S. Alley, "Television and Public Virtue," in Ferré, ed., *Channels of Belief*, p. 47.

54. Wildmon, *The Home Invaders*, pp. 18–22.

55. James B. Lemert, *Criticizing the Media: Empirical Approaches* (Newbury Park, CA: Sage Publications, 1989), p. 25.

56. S. Robert Lichter, Stanley Rothman, and Linda S. Lichter, *The Media Elite* (Bethesda, MD: Adler and Adler, 1986), p. 294.

57. Les Brown, *Television: The Business Behind the Box* (New York: Harcourt Brace Jovanovich, 1971), p. 15.

58. Ibid.

59. Cf., for example, Jacob Neusner, *Jews and Christians: The Myth of a Common Tradition* (London: SCM Press, 1991).

60. Newman, *Competition in Religious Life*, pp. 21–23.

61. Ibid., p. 22.

62. Ibid., p. 55. For detailed examples, cf. pp. 55–100, 148–73. On the complexity of salvation as a religious objective, cf. Newman, *On Religious Freedom*, pp. 178–80.

63. Cf. Newman, *Competition in Religious Life*, pp. 9–16.

64. Ibid., pp. 18–21.

65. Ibid., ch. 2.

66. Schultze, *Television: Manna from Hollywood?*, p. 156.

67. Postman, *Amusing Ourselves to Death*, p. 162.

68. Steve Bruce, *Pray TV: Televangelism in America* (London: Routledge, 1990), p. 196.

69. Michael R. Real, *Mass-Mediated Culture* (Englewood Cliffs, NJ: Prentice-Hall, 1977), p. 156.

70. Ibid., p. 268.

71. Matthew 5:39.

72. Matthew 28:19.

73. Cf. Newman, *On Religious Freedom*, pp. 94–123.

74. Ibid., p. 99.

75. Ibid., pp. 95–96.

76. Ibid.

77. Ibid., p. 27. Cf. ch. 4.

78. See Roger Bird, ed., *Documents of Canadian Broadcasting* (Ottawa: Carleton University Press, 1988).

79. Report of the Royal Commission on Radio Broadcasting (September 1929), in Bird, *Documents*, pp. 41–54.

80. Bird, Introduction to Document 9, in Bird, *Documents*, p. 37.

81. Report of the Royal Commission, in Bird, *Documents*, p. 53.

82. Board of Broadcast Governors, "Political and Controversial Broadcasting Policies," Part 2 (December 18, 1961), in Bird, *Documents*, p. 572.

83. Ibid.

84. Horsfield, *Religious Television*, p. 68.

85. Cf. Newman, *Foundations of Religious Tolerance*, pp. 104–10.

86. Cf. Real, *Mass-Mediated Culture*, pp. 10, 199, 268.

87. Lawhead, *Turn Back the Night*, p. 129.

88. Porter, *The Media*, p. 88.

89. Ibid., p. 78.

90. Department of Research and Education of the Federal Council of the Churches of Christ in America, *Broadcasting and the Public: A Case Study in Social Ethics* (New York: Abingdon, 1938), p. 196.

91. Steven Starker, *Evil Influences: Crusades against the Mass Media* (New Brunswick, NJ: Transaction Publishers, 1989), p. 140.

92. Alan Wurtzel and Stephen R. Acker, *Television Production*, 3rd ed. (New York: McGraw-Hill, 1989 [1979]), p. 523.

93. Ibid., pp. 523–24.

94. Ibid., p. 524.

95. Ibid.

96. Ibid.

97. Ibid., p. 526.

98. Ibid., pp. 526–28.

99. Ibid., pp. 528–33.

100. Ibid., pp. 533–53.

101. Sydney W. Head and Christopher H. Sterling, *Broadcasting in America: A Survey of Electronic Media*, 5th ed. (Boston: Houghton Mifflin, 1987 [1956]), ch. 11–13.

102. Horace Newcomb and Robert S. Alley, *The Producer's Medium: Conversations with Creators of American TV* (New York: Oxford University Press, 1983), p. xii.

103. Ibid., p. xi.

104. Ibid., pp. xi–xii.

105. Ibid., pp. 34–44.

106. Ibid., p. 168.

107. Ibid., p. 172.

108. Ibid., p. 72.

109. Wildmon, *The Home Invaders*, pp. 31, 36. It is instructive to constrast Wildmon's view of Lear with Alley's view of Lear as an "American moralist"; cf. Alley, *Television*, p. 133.

110. Newcomb and Alley, *The Producer's Medium*, p. 191.

111. Ibid., p. 193.

112. Muriel G. Cantor, *The Hollywood TV Producer: His Work and His Audience* (New Brunswick, NJ: Transaction Books, 1987 [1971]), pp. 3–4.

113. Ibid., p. 7.

114. Ibid., p. xxxv.

115. Ibid.

116. Ibid., p. 174.

117. Ibid., p. 173.

118. Ibid., p. 172.

119. Ibid., pp. 74–75.

120. Ibid., p. 204.

121. Ibid., p. 200.

122. Ibid.

123. Ibid., p. 201.

124. Ibid., p. 203.

125. Wurtzel and Acker, *Television Production*, p. 528.

126. Cantor, *The Hollywood TV Producer*, p. 208.

CHAPTER THREE

Religious Television

One reason why the expression "competition between religion and television" is apt to strike many people as strange is that it indirectly calls to mind religious television programming, which would appear to be evidence of cooperation between religion and television. One realizes on reflection, however, that religious television programming represents only one dimension of the complex relationship between religion and television. One may come to see that there is much programming on television that, while not appropriately characterized as religious, has some sort of religious significance, in, say, being imbued with religious values or attitudes. On further reflection, one may also arrive at the conclusion that religious television programming may actually be one of the areas in which television comes into competition with religion, or at least with "traditional" religion.

If we are to understand the general phenomenon of competition between religion and television, and the cultural controversies associated with it, we must obviously give some attention to religious television. We will begin with a consideration of religious television programming itself. When many people hear the words "religious television" or even "religion and television," they immediately think of televangelical programs. This is perhaps because they assume that most religious programs on television fit into this category. Peter G. Horsfield writes that, "In 1979 more than half of all national airings of religious programs were accounted for by only 10 major evangelical programs. Other religious expressions and traditions were almost forced off the air totally by these (now) wealthy conservative Protestant organizations."[1] I am not sure how reliable this statistic is, or how reliable most statistics in this field are, and I am not sure how much religious programming has changed since 1979. But no one who watches television in the United States, Canada, and many other Western societies will dispute the claim that the programs of major televangelists have come to represent a very large presence, if not a dominant one, in religious television programming. The enormous attention that these programs receive (relative to other forms of religious programming) from people who do not watch them is not simply a function of the number or proportion of such programs on the air, or even of the number of people who do watch them and are influenced by them. Some of the leading televangelists are quite unusual personalities who become involved in some rather strange events. For this reason among others they receive considerably more attention from the mass media than their blander colleagues in religious ministries on television and elsewhere. And the televangelists' programs themselves often leave a lasting impression, of a kind that other religious programs do not, on people who have only watched a few of them. They typically have a strangely theatrical quality, they involve curious and frequent appeals for money, and they often show large audiences of "simple" believers who strike the average television viewer as extraordinarily naive and gullible. So while much religious programming on television does not belong in this category, people should not be harshly criticized for immediately forming an image of the televangelist when the subject of religious television is broached.

It was not always this way. In the early years of television, televangelists did not have the great cultural presence that they now have. In the United States, the presence of syndicated evangelical programs broadcast on purchased time increased dramatically after 1970.[2] Television programmers themselves have actually promoted this form of religious programming, and in effect this form of religious "experience," as "local stations have found it more profitable to sell time to evangelical and fundamentalist syndicators than to provide free time for public-service programming."[3] Many leaders of mainstream churches have resented this, and have regarded it as a major example of unfair competition between television and mainstream religion.

In Steve Bruce's view, "American religious television is so obviously dominated by fundamentalists, evangelicals, and pentecostals that it requires conscious mental effort not to treat televangelism and religious television as synonyms."[4] But in explaining this state of affairs, Bruce does not place primary emphasis on the commercial interests of television executives and programmers. Like other students of the mass media that we considered in Chapter 1, Bruce is impressed by certain features of mainstream institutional religion that have to some extent made its characteristic presentation of its messages "unsuited to mass media".[5] The major televangelists are customarily ridiculed and dismissed by media critics and other sophisticated viewers, but the derision is often tinged with bigotry, and if Jeffery K. Hadden and Charles E. Swann are right, "The televangelists are destined to play a critical role in the shaping of the balance of the twentieth century. They have more undisputed access to the airwaves than any other social movement in American society."[6]

In the early years of television, representatives of the "establishment churches"[7] found themselves in much the same position as other people faced with a new technology; they were learning on the job and experimenting with various different approaches. In the United States, their situation was facilitated by the network sustaining-time system, which experienced a gradual demise in the 1970s.[8] Some of the approaches they developed are still employed today, and we shall consider these later. But over the years, the presence of the televangelists became more and more pronounced. Interestingly, the first great television preacher in America was not an Evangelical Protestant but a Roman Catholic educator, Fulton J. Sheen, whose television ministry was remarkably successful by many standards.[9] Bishop Sheen was a splendid figure in his magnificent robes, and he dispensed Thomistic wisdom to 1950s audiences with a remarkable flair. As the years passed, the Roman Catholic hierarchy did not quite know what to do with Sheen himself; but it clearly decided at some point that it wanted no more of Sheen's high style of television preaching. However, Protestant televangelism grew and grew, in some ways becoming more sophisticated. Although media critics and other "refined" viewers generally think of the televangelists as being more or less the same, one can distinguish various types. Thus, for example, Hadden and Swann refer to the "supersavers," such as Billy Graham, Oral Roberts, Rex Humbard, and Jerry Falwell;[10] the "talkies," such as Jim Bakker and Pat Robertson;[11] the "entertainers," such as Jimmy Swaggart;[12] the "teachers," such as Richard De Haan and Frank Pollard;[13] and the one notable "mainliner," Robert Schuller.[14] Although such typologies can be valuable, we should not forget that there are even more specific differences (in, for example, format and style) between the programs of individual televangelists (as, for example, between Roberts' and Falwell's, and between Bakker's and Robertson's), and we should be careful not to underestimate the importance of fundamental similarities.

Given the particular set of problems in cultural theory that we are addressing in this study, we may consider televangelism more generally and in less concrete detail than many other students of the phenomenon have, and when we do so, we will find that the programs of televangelists have much in common with the more traditional ministries of mainstream institutional religion, particularly mainstream Protestantism. Consider the basic content of these programs. The core is invariably

preaching. One or more religious ministers stands or sits before the television audience, and often also a live audience (normally a religious
congregation), and sermonizes. Each preacher draws upon Scripture and
supposedly related sources of spiritual insight to shed light on any number of personal moral weaknesses and social corruptions, to elucidate
and promote what he (or occasionally she) takes to be the foremost
means to personal improvement and social reform, and to provide consolation and encouragement to people that he or she assumes are in need
of both. Emphasis is placed on the authority of the sources that are being
cited and applied, but there is usually also a certain amount of secular
moral, philosophical, and scientific argumentation brought in to clarify
and strengthen the religious exhortation. Often there are musical numbers, and sometimes people from the live audience or special guests offer
something in the way of personal testimony. And there is almost invariably some form of fund-raising to support the continuing work of the
ministry.

Viewed in this light, what happens on these programs is not significantly different from what happens at most services in most mainstream
Protestant churches. Certain of its essentials have a great deal in common
with what happens at the religious service of most mainstream non-
Protestant religious denominations, too. And while a televangelical program may sometimes depart from this basic format and content, some
degree of novelty and experimentation can fairly be expected even in
mainstream religious services.

Why then are so many representatives of mainstream Protestantism
and mainstream institutional religion in general so critical of televangelical programs? More specifically, why do they see the particular alliance
of televangelists with television as posing a grave threat to genuine religion and authentic religious experience? When we scrutinize the main
arguments offered by these critics, we may well find that they are not
as compelling as the critics and their supporters take them to be.

The first main criticism is that for a variety of reasons the religious
teaching and the opportunity for religious experience that televangelical
programs offer are essentially superficial in comparison with what more
traditional forms of religious ministry generally offer. Critics thus complain, for example, that televangelical programs avoid doctrinal detail,[15]
offer little challenge to the values and practices of the secular world,[16]
lack any depth of social critique,[17] and focus on satisfying viewers' immediate needs rather than on transmitting the deep and complex message of the faith that they are promoting.[18] The second main criticism is
that televangelism is, for various sociological and technological reasons,
inextricably tied to a socially conservative agenda[19] that promotes values
that may contradict traditional and essential aspects of the Christian

faith.[20] A third line of criticism is that televangelism is ineffective. In Quentin J. Schultze's words, it "has been a dismal failure at evangelizing nonbelievers, at least partly because televangelists become more interested in building an organization than in saving souls."[21] Another criticism is that televangelism vitiates religious experience by substituting for the personal fellowship that it cannot provide[22] a personality cult built around the preacher as "star."[23] The glamour[24] that so often surrounds the televangelist, whether or not it involves the actual flaunting of wealth, power, and indulgence—as undoubtedly it often does—would appear to undermine the teaching and preaching functions of the ministry. Finally, while some close observers are convinced that televangelists are for the most part sincere in professing that their essential concern is religious,[25] other observers have an unshakable suspicion that most televangelists are more concerned with money and fame than with promoting the faith.

Each of these criticisms calls for individual examination, but first, we should note not only that they can overlap and blend in various ways but that they all at least indirectly implicate television itself—whether as a technology, an industry, or a form of experience—as largely responsible for the corrupt and unwholesome aspects of televangelical programming. Most critics of televangelism will grant that television is not wholly responsible for the failings of televangelism. Nevertheless, the corrupting influence of television upon genuine religion is a continuous if sometimes veiled theme running through the typical multidimensional indictment of televangelism. It will be useful in our analysis to lift the veil from time to time. Religious critics of televangelism, however, are sometimes quite explicit in identifying television itself as a major problem. So, for example, Stewart M. Hoover criticizes broadcasters in the electronic church who have "mimicked the methods of television,"[26] and Horsfield, who notes that many observers see current religious programs as "accommodating themselves to the demands of commercial television,"[27] suggests that, "Rarely in its long history has the Christian church been so closely tied to and dependent on an external organization over which it has so little control as it does when communicating through the medium of television."[28]

The charge of superficiality is probably the most basic of the various criticisms directed at televangelism, and undoubtedly what televangelism offers in the way of religious teaching and opportunities for religious experience is meager indeed in comparison with what people have been offered by other professed spiritual authorities. But when we do the appropriate comparing, and consider a broad range of conditions and circumstances, we may be led to make a more generous appraisal of televangelical programming than that made by its sophisticated critics. For one thing, there are, in William James' memorable expression, numerous "varieties of religious experience,"[29] and as each one is to some extent sui generis, ranking them may be a rather arbitrary business that reveals more about the biases of the critic than the quality of the experiences themselves. The very criteria by which the ranking is done may be quite arbitrary. Are we to focus more on intensity than consistency, on intellectual rigor than unworldliness, on commitment to radical social reform than scrupulousness in personal affairs? A case can be made for any of these criteria, but when one gets down to ranking individual believers and the value of their form of religious commitment, one invariably risks some degree of narrow-mindedness and unwarranted self-justification. The fact is that even some of those individuals taken to represent paradigms of the religiously profound individual, such as Augustine and Kierkegaard, have been more than a little hypocritical and somewhat mad, and are not the best role models for the typical believer. Moreover, televangelism appeals widely to people who are either incapable of or temperamentally disinclined toward such approaches to faith as the mystical, the philosophical, or the academic-theological. Thus it provides something in the way of spirituality to many people who might otherwise be unable to participate in spirituality and would be left with a form of materialism even less profound than a "superficial" religious commitment. Again, a certain form of religious commitment, say, a philosophical one, may be intellectually profound but emotionally shallow, so that the one-dimensional ranking of religious experiences may be simplistic and misleading. Excessive concern with doctrinal detail, in leading people away from a certain form of spiritual simplicity, may lead to the sort of foolishness and hypocrisy so well described in such works as Erasmus' *Praise of Folly*. Also, excessive concern with the radical-reformist socio-political aspects of religious commitment may lead one to reduce faith to political-ideological commitment.

Television itself is, of course, implicated in much of the criticism of the superficiality of televangelical programming. For even though critics of televangelism will often point to what they consider to be superior forms of religious television programming, in their attack on televangelism in particular they at least indirectly indicate what religious television as such cannot provide that other forms of religion can. Here we need only to think back to the arguments, considered in the first two chapters, that major dimensions of religion are not "televisible" or capable of being made accessible through television, and that the technological and commercial aspects of television inevitably result in a narrow and highly particularized form of religious involvement. However, even more "respectable" forms of religious involvement such as the mystical, philosophical, or academic-theological are narrow and highly particularized in their own right, and it is hardly surprising that most ordinary people, even when they have tried to be open to such forms of religious involvement, have simply been unable to get involved in them. It would have been nice to have seen more of deep religious thinkers like Martin Buber, Paul Tillich, Thomas Merton, Karl Rahner, and Mircea Eliade on television, but even if their lectures and interviews could have been made properly "televisible," it is not clear that they would have done much for most of the people who have stood to benefit from what televangelism offers.

Those old enough to remember the golden years of radio broadcasting may be tempted to contrast television unfavorably with radio with respect to the ability of the two forms of broadcasting to accommodate more learned and more serious religious broadcasters such as the thoughtful theologian-minister, Harry Emerson Fosdick, whose presentations I myself have heard and in various ways admired. I doubt that the salient consideration here is Marshall McLuhan's contrast between a "cool" medium and a "hot" one. The more relevant point here is that radio can be more suitable for relatively abstract presentations because it does not distract the listener with largely irrelevant visual imagery. What I have in mind specifically is a contemporary application of the famous argument of Plato, presented most vividly in the cave parable of the *Republic*, that enabling people to apprehend moral and other higher ideas requires freeing them to some extent from their reliance on sensory perception and its concrete data. Of course, listening to a theologian on the radio involves perception, as does even the reading of a book like the *Republic*, but on a very different level than watching television does, especially in light of the fact that the way one watches a preacher or theologian on television is conditioned by the way in which one has become accustomed to watching sports events, situation comedies, detective stories, and the like. However, given the way in which radio programming itself has developed in recent years—particularly with so much of it given over to pop music—and given broader cultural changes, we may question whether an approach like Fosdick's would be as effective on radio today as it was years ago. Also, we should recognize that talented producers, directors, and technicians have over the years increasingly demonstrated an ability to enable more learned and more serious religious teachers to transmit their message effectively on television—a matter we shall return to later. Finally, we should not forget that radio and not television has been the forum for the most influential of the fiery broadcasters, such as Father Charles Coughlin, who have exploited supposedly religious convictions in the promotion of hatred.

Televangelism cannot offer what the local congregation can in the way of personal fellowship. I am further prepared to grant that what the typical local clergyman offers in the way of teaching, guidance, and counsel is by many criteria superior to what the typical televangelist offers. Nevertheless, televangelism offers something irreplaceable not only to those who because of some disability are unable to participate actively in the life of a local congregation, but to many people who have participated in the life of a local congregation and found it to be lacking. The popularity of televangelical programs represents to some extent the repudiation of certain traditional religious institutions. Most people who watch televangelical programs on a regular basis have had extensive involvement at some point in their lives with traditional congregational activity, and a good many of them have been "turned off" by their experiences. That may be in part because they are somewhat indolent, irresponsible, or unimaginative. But it may also be because they have had enough of congregational politics, tedious and mechanical sermonizing, poor music, confusing theology, and the like. Then again, neither televangelism as such nor television in general demands that the viewer give up participation in local congregational life or any other activity that transcends the small screen. Perhaps television programmers can fairly be regarded as enticing viewers to loosen their ties to that outside world, but if the critic of televangelism or television in general insists in regarding typical viewers as wholly manipulable robots incapable of making reflective judgments and free choices, then he is probably a more dangerous force in society than the people whose excessive influence he denounces.

Having said that, I must reiterate that by my own criteria, what televangelists generally offer their audiences is meager compared to what many other religious teachers have historically offered, and what television programmers generally offer their audiences is meager compared to what they might instead be offering. It is not unfair to expect something better from these communicators, but we must bear in mind that at least a significant part of their determination of what to offer is based on judgments concerning what their targeted audience wants, needs, and can assimilate. They are, after all, communicators. Thus, to some extent the problem of the relative superficiality of televangelism, or of any television programming, is the problem of democracy itself. In the seminal work of classical philosophy of culture, the *Republic*, Plato makes a devastating (and still relevant) attack on the democratic system, with all its mediocrity, disorder, and artificial equality.[30] But Plato was too wise not to recognize that in the final analysis despotism is even worse than democracy.[31] Plato detested democracy because it is a system in which most people are free but only in a superficial sense, and so their much vaunted freedom inevitably degenerates into a license that prevents sound sociopolitical development of the kind needed to foster true freedom in the form of personal self-realization.[32] The struggle to bring about the religious liberty that most of us now enjoy was, as noted in Chapter 2, an arduous and generally noble one, but religious liberty entitles individuals to be religious in superficial as well as subtle and profound ways, and that is a bitter truth that the high-minded observer of culture must learn to swallow. It is estimable to want to free people from their pre-occupation with the shadows on the cave wall, but doing so requires immense patience, tact, and compassion rather than condescension and whining.[33]

If, however, televangelists are promoting a social agenda that is at odds with civilization and progress, that is quite another matter, and we can hardly afford to be permissive. And if some of its critics are right, then the larger part of televangelism is devoted to a social agenda that is conservative in the worst sense of the term: reactionary, intolerant, and promotive of the interests of the predatory and exploitative rather than the innocent and oppressed. If this criticism is sound, then televangelism is indeed at odds with civilization and progress, and with the very Christianity it professes to be promoting, a Christianity that teaches that the meek, merciful, and pure in heart are the salt of the earth and the light of the world.[34] The self-righteousness of most televangelists can indeed be appalling, but televangelists are, after all, preachers, and when they are not at their best, preachers of any kind have a way of drifting from astute and measured criticism to rancorous, bigoted, maleficent demagoguery. Television as such does not make televangelists more demagogical than other preachers, except insofar as it provides them with a forum in which they may see it as prudent to be more demagog-ical than they would otherwise be. However, it certainly makes them more dangerous than most demagogues, mainly because it enables them to reach a much wider audience than they could otherwise reach.

The label of "conservative" that is used by Steve Bruce[35] and others to designate the social agenda of leading televangelists is not entirely helpful, especially when it is used in a pejorative way similar to the way in which so many of the televangelists use the corresponding label "lib-eral" as a stick with which to beat those that they portray as agents of the devil. However, Bruce is undoubtedly right when he observes that the principal spokesmen of American televangelism "oppose abortion, homosexuality, sex education, and the Equal Rights for women Amend-ment to the constitution (ERA). The core of televangelism's socio-moral platform is the importance of the 'traditional' nuclear family."[36] He is also right to point to the "super-patriotism" of leading televangelists.[37] And there is undoubtedly much truth to the contention of many of the televangelists' critics that the leading televangelists manifest a remarka-ble indulgence toward the darker side of capitalism, for though almost all televangelists at least periodically promote compassion for the dis-advantaged both at home and abroad, they rarely if ever suggest that American-style capitalism is fundamentally flawed. If this is how we are to understand the claim that American televangelism generally promotes a socially conservative agenda, then the leading American televangelists are indeed socially conservative.

Many of the leading televangelists are wealthy, and some parade their wealth; they are not overtly worried about Jesus' words, "But woe unto you that are rich! for ye have received your consolation."[38] And though Jesus characterizes the meek and the poor as the light of the world, many leading televangelists readily make known their close association with those who possess worldly power. In his one-dimensional but usefully provocative study of Billy Graham, Michael Real suggests that the great evangelist is "strictly post-Constantinian in the ease with which he mixes with established world powers,"[39] and that, "On a more specific level, the variety of religion that Graham represents is a blend of Reformation Protestantism and economic capitalism."[40] What makes these points all the more significant is that Graham is one of the major televangelists least offensive to most social, political, and economic liberals. The conservative socio-political agenda of the leading televangelists is almost routinely tied to what many academic theologians would characterize as a conservative theology, specifically, fundamentalism or something akin to it. I cannot think of any good philosophical or theological reason as to why a conservative socio-political agenda should be seen as necessarily tied to a conservative theology, but perhaps a behavioral or social scientist could give a satisfactory psychological or sociological explanation. In any event, for most of the major televangelists, the linkage is plain. When critics of televangelism disparage the conservative theology of leading televangelists, it is ordinarily on the grounds that such theology is "superficial," but when they attack the conservative socio-political agenda of these televangelists, their criticism takes on a more universal character and a more severe tone.

While some of the socio-political propaganda of the leading televangelists strikes me as sinister and depraved, some of what they say about abortion and other subjects strikes me as morally sound. Perhaps I am more inclined than critics of televangelism to focus on the individual moral and political teachings of televangelists than on their socio-political agenda as a whole. I am not suggesting that critics of televangelism are wrong to focus on the televangelists' agenda as a whole, and in any case, this is not the place to examine in detail the individual moral and political teachings of leading televangelists. But having expressed a strong distaste for some of the socio-political propaganda of these people, I also consider it appropriate to try to say something in their defense.

First, before we indulge in the hyperbole of dismissing the socio-political agenda of the leading televangelists as rightwing extremism—loose talk about the "religious right" has been in fashion in certain mass media circles for some time now—we should note that the conservatism of the agenda is more appropriately associated with certain values of the lower and middle economic classes than with the principal values of wealthier people. Although the captains of industry and other representatives of the wealthier class may approve of much that televangelists preach and teach, the audience of televangelists is for the most part not particularly affluent, and it is not to the affluent that the televangelists make their primary appeal. Critics of the televangelists' socio-political agenda have themselves acknowledged this fact. Bruce, for example, sees the preaching of the televangelists as strikingly consistent with the way of life of "fairly conservative, lower middle-class, small-town Americans."[41] And these people, despite any special interest that they may have in such controversial social issues as abortion and homosexuality, seem to be at least as much concerned with the economic and foreign policy issues that concern the majority of their fellow citizens.[42] Moreover, televangelists and their followers are hardly the only North Americans who have grave doubts about the moral acceptability of such practices as homosexuality and abortion, or who are given to criticism of what they perceive as a certain liberal bias of most broadcasters. Even a good many people who consider themselves liberal and feel that their socio-political agenda is much closer to that of Norman Lear than that of Donald Wildmon have been known to worry about some of the very things that trouble televangelists and their viewers. In their criticism of the failings of capitalism, these people may not be all that more vocal than the televangelists. (Political radicals have frequently been more contemptuous of self-professed liberals than of self-professed conservatives; they often regard the former as more hypocritical.) Although he probably overstates the point, Schultze is not far off when he suggests that televangelism is a "characteristic" expression of American religion and that, "To criticize televangelism is to criticize the broader American cultural currents that gave birth to the phenomenon and are now so heavily influenced by it. Whether we like it or not, all of us are borne along by those currents, regardless of our values and religious backgrounds or experiences."[43] If Schultze is right, then not only televangelism but North American religion as such has been "steadily influenced by the values, attitudes, and beliefs that animate contemporary business life."[44] And of course, these values, attitudes, and beliefs have manifested themselves in other areas of culture, as, for example, in higher education and research, in sports, and in the fine arts.

Horsfield more specifically points to the problem of religious television's reflecting "the dominant values and social functions of commercial television."[45] Although this point applies to some extent to religious television programming in general, it would appear to apply even more to televangelism in particular, especially to the conservative socio-political agenda promoted by leading televangelists. We should hardly be surprised at this point to see television itself implicated, but the values and social functions of commercial television that trouble critics like Horsfield may not be very different from those in other cultural domains. High-minded though they may be in certain ways, many professors, novelists, journalists, and functionaries of mainstream religious institutions have an interest in preserving an economic status quo that has benefited them considerably.

Finally, simplistic and dogmatic though it may be in its essentials, the general socio-political agenda that is put forward by televangelists does at least have the virtue of being relatively clear, focused, stable, and cohesive, whereas that associated with liberalism often seems to lack these qualities.[46] The socio-political agenda of the major televangelists resembles their theology in this regard. Although much can be said in defense of liberal theology, it, too, leaves many religionists puzzled and confused and sometimes with a feeling of spiritual emptiness.[47] Televangelism and kindred developments in recent religious life have, in fact, been useful in encouraging the more reflective representatives of mainstream religion to "redefine themselves,"[48] or at least reconsider what precisely it is that they are trying to promote in contrast with what televangelists and others are promoting.

The general effectiveness of televangelism seems to me to be very difficult to assess. First, the criteria by which one could assess the effectiveness of televangelism are numerous, and the decision to concentrate on the application of one criterion at the expense of others will necessarily involve subjective factors. Second, the methods that might be employed to do the measuring here, such as survey research, are not entirely satisfactory. Even if televangelists were to agree that their basic aim is to win converts, they might disagree profoundly as to what and how much this involves, and to how we are to determine whether the type and degree of conversion specified has taken place. If Schultze is right in claiming that televangelists often "exaggerate their evangelistic data,"[49] the fact remains that they may do so not only to "maintain a facade of evangelistic outreach"[50] but because like most of us they favor that interpretation of the relevant data that is most compatible with a sense of self-worth and accomplishment. But the general question of whether watching televangelical programs makes one better—or better off—may be as difficult to answer objectively as the question of whether religion as such, or television as such, makes one better or better off.

Undoubtedly, televangelists are to a great extent involved in preaching to the converted, telling those who choose to watch what they want to hear and not necessarily what they need to hear. But professors, belletrists, journalists, broadcasters, and local clergymen all do a good deal of their preaching to the converted, which is an inevitable consequence of people having the freedom in societies like our own to choose what they are going to read, watch, and listen to. In any case, people do sometimes change their minds or even undergo conversion experiences. I for one am not prepared to dismiss people as naive, manipulable fools just because they believe that watching televangelical programs has significantly altered their lives.

When we turn to the criticism that televangelism vitiates religious experience by substituting for the personal fellowship that it cannot provide a personality cult built around the preacher as "star," we are faced with an issue that we considered earlier, the legitimacy of different varieties of religious experience. What I said earlier on applies here as well. We should consider that personal fellowship is not the sine qua non of authentic religious experience (as the case of the mystic strikingly illustrates); that televangelism provides some viewers with the closest thing to personal fellowship that, given their circumstances or temperament, they are likely to experience; and that the form of fellowship that televangelism provides, whatever its limitations, may be more satisfying or fulfilling to a certain individual than the form of fellowship encountered in a local religious congregation or community. However, when we consider the matter of televangelism's treatment of the preacher as star, and the matter of the glamour and slickness of televangelical programming, a new set of issues arises.

Here again television itself is implicated. Television is seen by critics as interfering with personal fellowship; parking oneself in front of the small screen, one is cut off from the world of genuine human relationships and, worst of all, from the intimate interaction that should characterize family life. Televangelical programming is a form of television programming, and is open to the general criticisms directed at television programming as such. But unlike other forms of religious television programming, televangelical programming is, many of its critics argue, brazenly mimicking the methods of commercial television, and this is nowhere more evident than in its treatment of the preacher as star.[51] One may recall at this point Neil Postman's general comments about religion and television. Postman also has a specific observation that is particularly relevant here:

Television's strongest point is that it brings personalities into our hearts, not abstractions into our heads.... And Jimmy Swaggart plays better than God. For God exists only in our minds, whereas Swaggart is *there*, to be seen, admired, adored. Which is why he is the star of the show. And why Billy Graham is a celebrity....[52]

And what of God? "[O]n television, God is a vague and subordinate character."[53]

These points are worth making, and they have more than a little truth to them. However, when we are finished with our indignant scoffing at the television star system and the televangelism that has ostensibly adopted it, we should proceed to take a closer look at the star system and its deep historical roots. It helps to remember right from the start that televangelism is not only a form of television but a form of religion, and that much of its character, despite those of its aspects that are not traditional, is derived from its religious nature. We have already taken note of Razelle Frankl's useful observation that, "The history of the electric church and the use of mass communications to preach the gospel can be traced to modern revivalism as developed in the nineteenth century;"[54] and, of course, it can be traced back much, much further. Indeed, when we think back to the beginnings of recorded history, we see that institutional religion has always been dominated by stars of various orders. At the top of the hierarchy we find God, or as some would have it, the "gods." Then there are the great prophets, and after them the lesser prophets and the saints. Of course, there are the priests of one sort or other, along with the sages of various kinds. There are the more notable, more influential, and more colorful among the functionaries of the various denominations and religious communities. And there are also various abstractions that become personalized to some extent, often in strange ways. The names are very familiar even to most people who have received little in the way of formal education: Jehovah, Moses, Elijah, Zeus, Buddha, Confucius, Jesus, Paul, Augustine, Mohammed, Luther, Pascal, Schleiermacher, John Henry Newman, Joseph Smith, Dwight Moody, Karl Barth, Pope John XXIII, Khomeini, Jimmy Swaggart, and so forth.

In considering the star system of traditional religion, we may be reminded that when religion is scrutinized from a utilitarian or pragmatic point of view, one of its main functions can be seen to be to provide individuals and communities with a conception of authority that can serve as a foundation for confidence in a worldview that will encourage socially constructive behaviour.[55] Given the natural human inclination to conceive of things in human terms, it is not hard to see why authority as such has usually been conceived primarily as something personal rather than purely abstract, even in cultures that have reacted against the cruder forms of anthropomorphic thinking. And any personal being that is conceived as a proper authority with respect to the highest matters, such as justice and truth, is a star. It is worth noting in this regard that a term now widely used to designate star quality in such fields as entertainment and politics, *charisma*, has its roots in Christian theology, for charisma was originally thought of as being divinely inspired, and in the theology of the apostle Paul was clearly associated with authority.[56] The concept of charisma has unquestionably been devalued in contemporary discourse,[57] and the stars of the current worlds of entertainment and politics rarely possess even a small fraction of the spiritual depth and significance of an Elijah, Paul, or even a Pascal or Schleier-macher. Even so, we should note that if television is to be seen as at fault here, it is not because television invented the star system, but because it has made it easier to regard as stars people who for various moral and practical reasons should not be regarded as such. And in doing the latter, it has merely followed one more tradition, that of hype and promotion. Its methods in this realm were clearly derived in large part from other mass communications media, most obviously from the cinema, but can be traced back by the student of the history of culture to promotional strategies employed by ancient competitors in intercultural and intracultural struggles, the most striking example being that employed in the propaganda of the early Christians.[58]

Religion is in important ways the most basic form of human culture and experience—and the ultimate source of major features of forms of culture and experience that are now conceived as essentially competitive with it. This is a theme we shall return to in the final chapter. We may note at this point, however, that as the sacred works of the world's major faiths have primarily taken the form of historical narrative rather than philosophy, institutionalized religion's emphasis on personalities rather than abstract principles is no mystery.

There would surely be stars in all cultural domains even without television, for even if people could get on without authority figures and role models, they apparently could not get on without invidious distinctions, pecking orders, ranks, ratings, and all the related paraphernalia by which the worth of a human being's life is assessed. And television certainly did not invent glamour or slickness, though it has transformed our conceptions of them in subtle ways. Furthermore, television has probably more often discovered and given exposure to stars than invented them outright. And some of the stars that it has paraded before its audiences have perhaps actually had charisma in the original sense of the term. If most of the televangelists and other celebrities that television pushes to the forefront of our culture generally lack the spiritual, moral, and intellectual qualities appropriate for the role models, heroes, teachers, and guides that our troubled civilization requires, then that is certainly to be regretted. Nevertheless, critics of television from the domains of institutionalized religion, higher education, and the fine arts have generally not made enough of an effort to get their own houses in order, and few among them have taken a hard look at the foolish star system that infects their own vocation. I have yet to be persuaded that there is more slickness to a Jimmy Swaggart or a Billy Graham than to a Martin Heidegger, Paul Tillich, or John Paul II; nor am I convinced that the slickness of either of the former has been more maleficent than that of any of the latter.

The supposed slickness and glamour of televangelists and their min-

istry may themselves be called into question. Even when a relatively
urbane televangelist like Pat Robertson substitutes for fiery preaching
and faith healing an ostensibly Christianized version of broadcast news
and political commentary, he has nothing of the smoothness of the typical network news anchor. And what is the slickness of an Oral Roberts
compared to that of the typical talk show host? For all the talk about the
ministries of televangelists like Roberts mimicking the methods of commercial television, the style and content of the typical televangelical program strike most people, including most Christian believers, as rather
crude and even silly. We might just as well ask what the slickness of an
Oral Roberts is compared to that of the typical Oxbridge theology professor or the clever young cleric down the street with his degree from
Notre Dame or Union Theological Seminary.

We are left, then, with the criticism that televangelists are generally
more concerned with money and fame than with promoting the faith.
This is an enormous generalization, and if it is overstated, then it is a
rather hateful and treacherous calumny. Even if it is not overstated, it
can be extremely misleading, for it does an injustice to the few earnest
televangelists who are indicted along with the venal pack. Every scandal
involving a televangelist inevitably damages the respectability and reliability of televangelism in general. As religious critics of televangelism
are well aware, it to some extent damages the respectability and reliability of religionists in general. But one of the keys to avoiding intolerance and prejudice is judging people as individuals and not simply as
member-representatives of groups. And one of the keys to avoiding the
cynicism that is the most poisonous of vices is to work hard at assessing
one's fellows in the spirit of the teacher who enjoined his followers,
"Judge not, that ye be not judged."[59] To be sure, one cannot be a morally
responsible individual if one is not prepared to be morally indignant
when appropriate. Televangelists and other preachers who make it their
business to be more indignant than the rest of us leave themselves open
to more severe criticism than more indulgent souls. Still, as there would
appear to be nothing essentially corrupt in televangelism as such, the
moral failings of individual televangelists are hardly more philosophically significant than the moral failings of their critics, though if a substantial and incontrovertible pattern of venality among televangelists did
manifest itself, it would certainly be something to reckon with.

Although much of what has been said above may be regarded as con-
stituting a defense of televangelism, we have been interested not in televangelism for its own sake but rather in any light that can be shed on
the general phenomenon of competition between religion and television.
We also seek to explore the cultural controversies associated with it by
a critical examination of the major arguments that representatives of

mainstream religion offer in order to establish that the alliance of televangelists with television poses a grave threat to genuine religion and authentic religious experience. Televangelical programming is generally the most conspicuous if not the most important form of religious television programming at this time, and the significant presence of any form of religious television programming would initially appear to indicate a major form of cooperation between religion and television that counters the thesis that the relationship between religion and television is essentially competitive. But if the religious critics of televangelism are right, then we will be able to discern that this enormously popular form of religion that television has made possible, and indeed fostered, represents a prodigious rival and perhaps a virulent threat to genuine or authentic forms of religion and religious experience that are incompatible with television as experience, technology, and commercial enterprise. The contention here is that the most conspicuous form of religious television programming represents one of the most important ways in which television is in competition with religion, for even if televangelism is to be regarded as a form of religion, it is evidence of television's power to subvert, debase, and subjugate religion in its purer, traditional forms.

Our primary concern, then, has been with the attack on televangelism made by its religious critics, or at least by cultural critics who profess to respect "the best of religion,"[60] who concentrate a large part of their attack on television itself. The inadequacy of their main arguments is revealing. Televangelical religion, it now appears, is not nearly as superficial, bigoted, ineffective, slick, manipulative, and phony as its religious critics would generally have us believe. Whatever its failings, and these are indisputably profound, it is not necessarily worse than most traditional forms of religion, at least by the criteria that religionists themselves ordinarily apply. It is not necessarily less pure a form of religion, and it is not necessarily less appropriately characterized as "religion." As this is the case, then the charge that television is promoting televangelism at the expense of other forms of religion, and is corrupting religion and thus competing against it in a subversive manner, is rather hollow.

The judgment that television is promoting televangelism at the expense of other forms of religion is itself highly questionable. Granted, television stations have often found it more profitable to sell time to televangelists than to provide time free for other forms of religious programming.[61] And there may even be some television programmers who promote televangelism as a way of making religion seem as silly as possible. Furthermore, to the extent that the religion that televangelism offers is more "televisible" than other forms of religion, television as technology can fairly be said to be fostering it. Still, when one scrutinizes the tone as well as the content of religious criticism of televangelism, one should eventually be able to see that the fundamental and significant competition that is taking place here is not between religion and television but between rival forms of religion that involve competing theologies and competing socio-political agendas. In relation to this fundamental competition, the role of television is purely instrumental.

Most people actively involved in televangelical ministries are well aware of this competition, and their attitude toward it complements other major aspects of their worldview. As Razelle Frankl observes:

In addition to the use of any appropriate means to win souls, members of the electric church value the dynamics of a free-market economy in modern life, including competition for religious beliefs. They believe that the free market will recalibrate the economic system and the religious system and, because of this strongly held mindset, they claim to oppose federal government regulation and intervention. Despite their rejection of Darwinism, they equate successful competition with worthiness and confidently compete with other religious groups and organizations. One way they compete is by reaching out to those evangelicals who are nonaffiliated or disenchanted with their congregations.[62]

Representatives of mainstream institutional Protestantism and mainstream institutional religion in general are prepared to compete, too. Their attack on televangelism is not merely intellectual and spiritual; it is a practical effort to undermine a form of religion that they not only regard as impure or superficial but that they rightly recognize as undermining to some extent what they themselves represent and constantly endeavor to promote. Their interest in the viability and survival of an alternative form of religion is a highly personal one, involving an existential commitment and in many cases a vocation and a measurable social presence. In attacking televangelism's curious alliance with television, they score major points in their competition with televangelism and with conservative religion in general, for television is a convenient scapegoat. Their strategy here is all the more effective insofar as televangelists themselves routinely attack the television industry (and ironically, in the process, bite the hand that feeds them). Though not as fiercely competitive as their rivals in televangelism, they manage to get in their licks, in subtle and sometimes rather devious ways. And they survive. But faced with mounting evidence that they are falling behind their rivals in influence, fame, and number of followers, they sometimes turn cranky in a way that is ultimately counterproductive, and at the same time their antipathy toward television becomes increasingly irrational.

It is consoling to such people to believe that their failure to compete as successfully as they would like with their rivals in televangelism and conservative religion can be blamed largely on television. For if television is the primary cause of their failure, then they themselves cannot fairly be regarded as primarily responsible for that failure. But this rather deterministic attitude, like almost all flights to determinism, is basically unwholesome, as it functions as a disincentive to vigorous, creative, assertive action, particularly in a competitive encounter. So, for example, if the religion that they seek to promote is insufficiently "televisible," it is their proper task to work at making it such, without, of course, compromising its integrity in the process.

They will be helped in this regard if they acknowledge that religious television programming has always been rich in its diversity. Before they move to bold and risky experimentation, they should take stock of at least the major nontelevangelical forms of religious television programming that have long been made available to them, some of which have been utilized with considerable success even from the earliest days of broadcasting. But to be capable of doing so, they will have to abandon any consoling delusions about television.

Any number of typologies can be employed to distinguish and categorize the various kinds of religious television programming. The number and kind of typologies that one applies will reveal a great deal about how much knowledge and understanding one has of current religious television programming; how much knowledge and understanding one has of the history of religious television programming; how imaginative one is in conceiving of possible developments in religious television programming; and perhaps most importantly, what one regards as the most important aspects of religious television programming. Such aspects include format, style, perceived function, targeted audience, theological orientation, socio-political agenda, sponsorship, sources of funding, denominational association (including both the particular denomination itself if there is one, and the extent to which the program is sanctioned by the denomination's leadership or by specific intradenominational groups), length and frequency of presentations, budget and quality of production values, and accessibility (i.e., the number of stations on which the program is shown, and whether it is accessible through one or more of the following: free broadcast television [network or local stations], basic cable television, pay TV stations). This list indicates how much subjectivity necessarily enters into the determination of what constitutes an important typology. Furthermore, most items on the list are subject to a wide latitude of interpretation, so that, for example, such things as format and style may or may not be seen as involving, say, the degree of involvement of a live audience, the degree to which lay preachers are employed, and the relative degree to which live rather than videotaped material is used.

When we considered the typology applied to televangelism by Hadden and Swann, we noted that while such a typology can be useful, it can obscure what may conceivably be more important differences and can lead us to underestimate the significance of more important similarities. The list of conceivably important aspects of religious television programming that I have just presented indicates that my earlier caveat about the limitations of such a typology was, if anything, understated. Indeed, questions may arise as to whether a particular form of religious television programming is properly regarded as an example of televangelism at all, and if so, to what extent. Even being paradigmatically televangelical may not be as important a feature of a religious television program as is widely assumed. Obviously, much depends on the objectives of the person offering the typology—particularly on whether the typology is meant to be of general, wide-ranging value or simply to address a specific concern in a relatively narrow context.

With these points in mind, we can see how futile it would be for me to attempt to provide a comprehensive survey of even the major types of nontelevangelical religious television programming. In a sense, my list speaks for itself. When one gives more than passing consideration to each of the items on that list, one will not only be able to appreciate more deeply the extraordinary diversity of religious television programs but should be able to recall many different religious television programs and to recognize how distinctive each one was. Still, a few examples are in order.

You will probably recall having seen from time to time a traditional religious service on television. It may have been a lengthy and rather grandiose one, such as a Christmas Mass from the Vatican, the wedding of a prince, or the funeral of a president or prime minister. Or it may have been a regular congregational service not unlike local congregational services. (The Canadian Broadcasting Corporation has for many years broadcast on Sundays a different local congregational service each week; in addition to all sorts of Christian services, non-Christian services have sometimes been presented.) It may have been a small but absorbing excerpt from a seasonal holiday service shown on a local news program, somewhere between the daily sports and weather reports. Local news programs routinely show at the appropriate time of year a bit of the Jewish Passover Seder and the Orthodox Easter service, and sometimes they are more adventurous, introducing the religious rites of Muslims, Sikhs, aboriginal peoples, and witches. Notice that in contrast with paradigmatically televangelical programs, these programs or news items are not conceived in relation to the proselytizing aspirations of a particular religious community, are directed to a greater extent at viewers of many different faiths and of no faith at all, are not overtly concerned with the promotion of a socio-political agenda, and as a general rule are not funded by a particular religious institution.

You will probably also recall having tuned in to a regularly scheduled program that endeavors to promote understanding of different faiths, to promote interfaith dialogue and tolerance, and to present a wide variety of religious and theological opinions and perspectives. These programs offer preaching only in an attenuated form. Many of them are produced under the auspices of the news and public affairs department of a major commercial or public network or one of its local affiliates, sometimes in conjunction with a nondenominational or interdenominational group of academic religious studies scholars.

Then, of course, television regularly presents motion pictures (including made-for-television movies) and dramatic specials whose religious subjects or themes are so pronounced that they clearly qualify as religious television programs. One may immediately call to mind the Biblical epics of Cecil B. DeMille, more sophisticated if somewhat ponderous films like *The Song of Bernadette*, *The Robe*, *The Inn of the Sixth Happiness*, and *The Greatest Story Ever Told*, and lighter but in some ways more moving films like *Green Pastures*, *Here Comes Mr. Jordan*, and *Going My Way*. These are but a few of the dramatic shows built around religious subjects and themes that commercial and public television stations in North America regularly deliver to their audiences. In addition, more than occasionally an episode in a regularly scheduled dramatic or comedy series focuses on a religious theme or issue. I am reminded in particular of the sensitive if somewhat provocative treatment of religious subjects in episodes of series singled out for special criticism by Wildmon, *M*A*S*H* and Norman Lear's *All in the Family*.

We have already noted that general news programs do not ignore religious matters and events of special religious significance. While reporting and analysis in this area have left much to be desired by serious viewers, much the same can be said for most news coverage by commercial and public stations. So not only should we attach considerable importance to the observation of a scholar like Judith M. Buddenbaum that, "Network newscasts devote more attention to religion than critics imagine,"[63] but we should also bear in mind that the mess that commercial and public news broadcasters so often make of their coverage of religious matters roughly parallels the mess that they often make of their coverage of other matters—politics, economics, science, medicine, and the fine arts. Although television news coverage of religion is essentially news programming and is not primarily inspired by religious motives, some of its offerings do represent a kind of religious television programming, such as the outwardly pious features presented during the Christmas and Easter seasons or the features that provide a forum to prominent religious leaders and their opinions. It is useful to contrast the coverage of religion in this regard with that of philosophy, which is almost negligible in North America, though a bit more frequent in certain European countries.

In the early years of American television broadcasting, it was actually common for television stations to begin and end their programming with a brief "sermonette" offered each day by a different local cleric from one of the larger and more influential denominations. To my knowledge, no station in North America ever offered a forum of this kind to a secular humanist or anyone seeking to persuade the audience that religion is by and large a lot of detrimental hokum.

I am not denying here that over the decades commercial and public television stations could and should have offered more, better, and more diverse religious programming. Still, we should remember that through the years, especially in the early years of television when mainstream denominations actually had available to them a network sustaining-time system,[64] there were many lost opportunities, because mainstream clerics did not know quite how to utilize the new medium, because much of what they attempted to offer was not "televisible," and because even the best that they had to offer was simply not as interesting even to the typical religious viewer as other television programs, religious experiences, and activities. We should also bear in mind that every so often religious fanatics who have abused the television medium have sent a powerful message to public interest groups about the need to maintain pressure on government regulators and other public officials to protect religious minorities and other groups and individuals who stand to be victimized by such abuses.

With the spectacular advances in telecommunications technology in recent years, and the promise of even more remarkable advances to come, the situation has been gradually changing. There are exciting new opportunities for the promoters of nontelevangelical forms of religious broadcasting. Along with the advent of new technologies, government regulators have instituted somewhat more flexible policies with respect to religious broadcasting, and there have been signs of a more positive attitude toward religion in many circles as a result of increasing discontent with the virtual institutionalization of materialistic ideas and values in certain fields of contemporary culture. But in the last analysis, the promoters and producers of religious television programming will still have to establish that they have something sufficiently worthwhile and engaging to offer to both high-minded and less reflective viewers.

The wide range of religious programming offered on Canada's VISION TV, which began broadcasting in September 1988, is an impressive example of how television and religion can be creatively brought together on many levels. VISION TV, conceived by its operators as a "national multi-faith and multicultural network" that offers "television for the spirit,"[65] was licensed by the government regulatory agency under fairly specific Conditions of Licence[66] meant to prevent the kind of abuses mentioned above and discussed in some detail in Chapter 2.[67] One aspect of its programming mandate is to "provide paid access time to faith communities and broadcast ministries."[68] Thus, the network offers a wide variety of televangelical programs, but also offers many non-televangelical programs sponsored by mainstream Christian ministries and non-Christian religious communities. VISION TV programs have featured such televangelists as Kenneth Copeland, James Robison, Jack Van Impe, John Wesley White, Jerry Falwell, and Paul B. Smith. Among other offerings have been such programs as *Dhur Ki Bani* (a Sikh religious program), *Orthodox Voice*, *Reflections on Islam* and *TV Asia* (a Sikh, Hindu, and Muslim inter-religious show).[69] The network also produces its own programs, many of which involve the promotion of interfaith dialogue. It obtains for broadcast religious and quasi-religious programs of many kinds, including movies and documentaries, from a wide variety of sources, including the Canadian Broadcasting Corporation and the National Film Board of Canada. The network has been required by Condition of Licence to offer an extensive amount of network-produced and other programming *about* religion, "so-called 'values-based' fare designed to appeal to persons of all religious beliefs" and "intended to create a balanced forum for the discussion of religious life in Canada."[70] The programs it offers in this category are in fact often classifiable as religious, though they are very different indeed from televangelical programs and other programs that concentrate on proselytizing. So, for example, in one particular month, VISION TV offered special programs on children of the survivors of the Holocaust, the struggle of the Mohawks of Akwesasne against corporations dumping toxic waste into the St. Lawrence River, how people with the AIDS virus cope with the disease, Lubavitch Hasidim in Brooklyn, and a Muslim social worker in South Africa. It also offers regularly scheduled programs featuring interviews with spiritual leaders and social reformers, panel discussions of social problems, religious music, and short documentary features. Some high-brow movies and British series are thrown in to round out the schedule.

Some of the programing on VISION TV is self-righteous, manipulative, superficial, or poorly crafted, but much of it is also well conceived, earnest, stimulating, and uplifting. In any case, the network certainly offers, as it claims, the "radically different alternative" to the general fare provided by other networks.[71] The range of religious programs that it offers is particularly impressive, although interestingly enough, virtually every type of religious or quasi-religious program that it presents has been presented before on ordinary commercial and public television stations, and the prototype of some dates back to the earliest days of North American television. If the programs presented on VISION TV are generally superior to their ancestors, most of which are now largely forgotten, that is in large part simply because of superior production values. The producers of the latest programs know much more than the pioneers did about the technology and the craft—and maybe even about religion itself—and it shows. If the programs presented on VISION TV and comparable networks in other countries attract more and more viewers and earn more and more critical acclaim, it is likely that more high-quality religious programming will soon appear on other networks.

Our investigation of religious television, and its relation to cultural competition and cooperation between religion and television, has focused thus far on religious television programming. We have noted, however, that there may well be a religious dimension even to much television programming that would be more appropriately regarded as secular rather than religious. This point has been made by cultural theorists and cultural critics in different ways. When we reflect on it, we realize that some peculiar conceptual problems arise concerning the precise relationship between the religious and the secular.

Although a useful distinction can be made between religious television programming and secular television programming, the latter is often in important ways imbued with religious values and attitudes, and on this level may be regarded as to some extent religious. Insofar as secular television programming is religious in this sense, it represents cooperation between religion and television rather than competition between them. Thus, in the 1938 report, *Broadcasting and the Public*, which we considered in Chapter 1, the group of Christian researchers examining radio broadcasting had no difficulty recognizing that, "Much of the current broadcasting which carries no religious label has definitely religious values."[72] This point applies as much to television as to radio. And Horsfield, ever mindful of the possible hazards involved in the church's adaptation of television's use to the church's purpose,[73] goes so far as to suggest that, "Given the dominant functions of television in status conferral and image creation, religious uses of television may more effectively be achieved through secular programming than through religious programming."[74]

Horsfield's suggestion seems almost ironic. Can it really be that the most effective religious uses of television, and the most significant form of religious television, involve secular rather than religious programming? Implicit in such a suggestion is the idea that for the most part television programming is already religious enough, or potentially so, without earnest but misguided religionists getting involved in the risky business of making it more obviously religious. Whatever we may think of this idea, we should not have much trouble understanding how certain kinds of programming that were not intended as religious are imbued with religious values and attitudes and can serve as effective means for transmission of traditional religious messages. Not all secular programming has this religious import. The religious significance of an ordinary weather report, a documentary on recent astronomical discoveries, or a televised bikini contest is rather attenuated. But where higher values lie just beneath the surface of television programming, as they so often do, the influence of religion can reasonably be suspected. Of course, there are philosophers who would contend that the higher values are not as intimately connected with religion as religionists generally assume. These philosophers would stress the relation of higher values to reason or perhaps instinct, and would argue that while religion has traditionally been the primary instrument for promoting them, it is not the basic source from which they are derived. Nonetheless, these values have traditionally been associated with religion and were so associated long before human beings had any clear conception of *logos*, reason, or rationality. Furthermore, much secular television programming assumes and indirectly promotes certain metaphysical ideas long associated with, if not ultimately derived from, Western monotheistic religion, such as free will and moral responsibility, spirit-body dualism, life after death, purposiveness in nature, and the meaningfulness of human existence.

Television did not emerge in a vacuum; it was not created ex nihilo. Television is a cultural product created by human beings, and so, too, is every television program. While we can appreciate the observations of cultural theorists like Marshall McLuhan who see people as initially overwhelmed by new technologies, particularly those technologies that involve new forms of perception, we can also see that the human beings who create television programs are creatures of their culture and the heirs to age-old cultural traditions. Some of them are more aware than others of the powerful influence of traditional cultural ideas, values, and attitudes on their worldview and on their own cultural efforts. Some of them, though not many, actually work at undermining the influence, in their own lives as well as the lives of others, of particular aspects of traditional culture. But most people in the latter category nevertheless accept certain traditional cultural ideas, values, and attitudes as fundamentally sound, and see it as part of their vocation to promote those ideas, values, and attitudes among children and among those adults who do not hold them. Perhaps more importantly, they routinely promote those ideas, values, and attitudes without being aware that they are doing so.

Though we should not underrate their creativity and imagination, we must realize that the inventors of television and the first television programmers were on the whole not brilliantly original cultural theorists. As Robert Sobel observes:

[T]elevision developed within a pre-existent business structure and did not have to create one of its own. The same was true of the art, at least for the first few years. In effect, television was the child of radio, motion pictures, and the press, and in its early days adapted the forms and contents of these to suit its own technology and requirements.[75]

The chain of influence can be traced back much further; the earliest radio programmers, film producers and makers, and publishers and print journalists were themselves heirs not only to a particular business structure but to an enormous complex of traditional cultural institutions and perspectives. In both their personal and professional lives, they lived off the capital of traditional culture—more specifically, a traditional culture that was in extremely important ways a religious one.

Consider now a typical piece of secular television programming, such as a detective story or an episode of a situation comedy that does not directly address religious themes. Even if the emphasis is on provoking thrills or laughter, there is often plenty of moralizing going on; the bad guys are contrasted with the good guys, and the latter manifest certain traditional virtues, such as compassion, to a degree that the former do not. The good guys almost always win in the end, and even when they do not, they at least lose in a morally edifying way and win our sympathy, affection, and respect. We identify with them and want to be like them. Moreover, our attention has probably been directed, if rather subtly, to such things as the significance of an individual human life, the need for personal responsibility, the superiority of justice to prudence, the corruptive influence of such vices and sins as lust and avarice, and the availability of redemption. It may help in this regard to think back to some of the themes that producer Quinn Martin saw himself as integrating into his detective stories and other entertainment shows, such as, "Good conquers evil," and, "Nice guys don't have to finish last."[76]

Looking over his career as executive producer of the famous Western series *Gunsmoke*, John Mantley observed that his favorite episodes of the show were those that "said something about the human condition."[77] When interviewed by Newcomb and Alley, Mantley clearly took special pride in an episode of the series entitled "The Golden Land," an episode that won a major award from the National Conference of Christians and Jews. When reflecting on work other than his own, he singled out the detective comedy *Barney Miller* for its poignant treatment of human interaction and such themes as inhumanity, tenderness, and compassion.

Most religious media critics will freely grant that there is something spiritually sound or uplifting about certain entertainment shows that are not specifically religious. Such critics see a close connection between religion and morality, and are not impressed by the efforts of aggressive secularists to set up an impenetrable wall between the two. Thus, it would not strike most observers as strange to find a Christian media critic like J. Brent Bill praising the popular situation comedy *The Cosby Show* for encouraging us "to look at the sunny side of our own fami-

lies,"[78] or praising the thoughtful historical-dramatic series *Roots* for re-
minding us of "our heritage and shortcomings."[79] Bill gives special attention to *Surviving*, a show about two adolescents who commit suicide
together, and notes that such a show raises important questions with
which the whole family needs to deal. He also praises the network that
aired *Surviving* for having its Community Relations department put together and distribute a booklet on the problem of adolescent suicide, and
adds that, "[T]hough the networks often seem to only want a chance to
sell products, they do at times put morality before money."[80] Perhaps
even more interesting is Bill's ability to see something of value in soap
opera:

While soap people hardly behave in ways we [Christians] find acceptable, they
vividly portray how many folks are searching for more out of life. Soaps should
remind us of the lonely, searching people we know. Then perhaps we can come
up with ways of helping them before they become as desperate as their heart-
broken heroes.[81]

We can identify with the good guys or be moved by the plight of
"lonely, searching people" without being religious in a conventional
sense, perhaps simply because we are basically moral and considerate
and have come to be so on the basis of intuitions or rational, moral-
philosophical reflections. We should think twice, however, before dismissing the influence on our worldview of traditional cultural ideas,
values, and attitudes or choosing to ignore the religious character of
culture itself in its earliest and most basic form.

Lest we forget that the idealization of compassion and respect for individual human life is not simply natural, we would do well to contrast
the values with which most television dramatic and comedy programming is imbued with what Friedrich Nietzsche characterizes as the natural values that Western monotheism has undermined:

The slave's eye is not favorable to the virtues of the powerful: he is skeptical
and suspicious, *subtly* suspicious, of all the "good" that is honored there—he
would like to persuade himself that even their happiness is not genuine. Con-
versely, those qualities are brought out and flooded with light which serve to
ease existence for those who suffer: here pity, the complaisant and obliging hand,
the warm heart, patience, industry, humility, and friendliness are honored—for
here these are the most useful qualities and almost the only means for enduring
the pressure of existence.[82]

"At the risk of displeasing innocent ears I propose: egoism belongs to
the nature of a noble soul—I mean that unshakable faith that to a being
such as 'we are' other beings must be subordinate by nature and have
to sacrifice themselves."[83] A religious critic of commercial television

could fairly observe that some television programming does on one level glorify power and promote egoism, but if one takes a wide perspective, one sees that most dramatic and comedy programming is "moralistic" in the sense that Nietzsche found most objectionable.

Consider another major type of secular television programming, the broadcasting of professional sports events like baseball and hockey games. At first it might seem more difficult to regard games of this kind as imbued with religious values and attitudes than to regard most dramatic and comedy programs. Yet as Howard S. Slusher has pointed out, "The splendor of institutional religious life symbolized by clergy, temples, laws, and literature is comparable to commissioners, stadiums and arenas, rules of the game and an extensive heritage of truth and folklore."[84] Moreover, "Sport, as religion, is a form of *symbolic* representation of meaningful realities."[85] Michael Real, in the course of his attack on mass-mediated culture, discusses the "mythic functions of media sports"[86] and cites as an example how the Super Bowl telecast conveys a "feeling of larger-than-life drama."[87] Real is disturbed by how mass-mediated culture "tends to profane a civilization's most sacred and powerful words and images," and yet is impressed by how "in the process it manages to elevate otherwise mundane events of no real consequence to the status of spectacles of a powerful, quasi-sacred myth and ritual nature."[88] While granting that television coverage of professional sports is generally excessive and often rather preposterous, I would say of the best of this coverage what I have said elsewhere of high-quality sports journalism—that in concentrating on the human element in sports events and relating sports to other aspects of life, it can usefully draw our attention to the many ways in which such activity is related to values. Some of the archetypal figures on whom it focuses correspond to types that we encounter in sacred works and religious literature.[89] Many sports broadcasters do habitually make heroes out of worthless bums, but there are, to be sure, authentic sports heroes, even in the most highly paying professional sports, and many of the professional athletes who fall short of being heroic are adequate role models for viewers, especially younger ones. Television and other mass media can be reproved for generally glorifying professional athletes at the expense of better role models and people more deserving of our attention. Still, it is an overstatement to say that sports events or the accomplishments of athletes are of no real consequence. The importance—partly religious—attached to athletic activity in an imposing culture like that of the ancient Greeks is not to be taken lightly by the cultural theorist. It is noteworthy that many professional athletes are deeply religious people. Evidence of their religious commitment is not confined to their comments on television interviews but is more substantially revealed in their prodigious charitable works. Finally, the ideal of sportsmanship that is often emphasized in television coverage of professional sports events has affinities with various ethical ideals traditionally promoted by religious teachers.

If one surveys the television listings for any week it will not be easy to find more than a couple of shows (as opposed to commercials) that actually advocate or promote materialism, determinism, or even hedonism. There is, of course, plenty of sex and violence in television programming, particularly in North America. Almost all of this sex and violence, however, is routinely blended with moralism and sentimentalism. The teenage prostitutes, exotic artists, syndicate gangsters, and racist skinheads who appear on shows like those hosted by Geraldo Rivera may satisfy a desire of certain audiences to be frightened, thrilled, or titillated, but on a deeper level they arouse revulsion or pathos of a sort that makes most people grateful that their own lives, and the lives of those that they are bringing up, are more dignified and more proper. Certain characters on a melodramatic soap opera like *The Young and the Restless* have a steady stream of strange romantic involvements and threats to their life of a kind that few of us will experience even once or twice in a lifetime. While viewers may be fascinated by the melodrama, those same viewers usually also appreciate the moral and emotional distance between themselves and the characters, and the writers and directors have made it easy enough for them to do so. There are shows such as *Baywatch* that seem to many critics to exist for no better purpose than to provide audiences with the opportunity to watch beautiful young people frolic in skimpy bathing suits. That, after all, may not be such an insignificant purpose, especially in a world filled with so much ugliness and drabness. Yet if one intently watches an episode of such a series right through to the end, one will probably find that even here the story does not glorify materialism or hedonism but actually touches upon themes concerning such qualities as responsibility, loyalty, fairness, and prudence. It is almost as if one cannot escape the moralism and sentimentalism. Putting up with the moral messages may seem to be a price that one is forced to pay in order to be allowed to watch attractive people cavort on the beach; without the story, watching those people would not be very interesting for very long.

As a final example, consider the popular prime-time cartoon series *The Simpsons*. This series, designed at least as much for adult viewers as for younger viewers, pokes fun at all sorts of human foibles and even at some cherished cultural institutions. It effectively gilds whatever moral-philosophical pills it dispenses and makes them easy to swallow. In its treatment of institutionalized religion, it can be rather bold, capturing the absurdity not only of religious hypocrisy but even of certain ordinary religious attitudes and rites. Yet its scripts generally treat participation in institutional religious activity as a normal and ordinary part of life in American society, and the most sensible and amiable of the series' major characters, mother Marge, is the character who regularly emphasizes the importance of religion in family life. However hard the scripts may sometimes be on the inauthentic moralism of the outwardly pious type of person, they routinely convey the message that the moral-philo-sophical core of traditional Western religious teaching is fundamentally sound and the appropriate basis of American culture.

We should not conclude from any of this that there is no value in distinguishing between religious television programming and secular television programming. This distinction is still useful in indicating the primary emphasis of a specific program or type of programming, par-ticularly with respect to the intentions of its creators and promoters. But the religious import of much television programming that is fundamen-tally secular needs to be considered if we are to assess properly the religious critic's contention that television is a great cultural rival of tra-ditional and authentic religion.

So far, however, we have considered only the simplest version of the thesis that much secular television programming has an important reli-gious dimension. We turn now to the more provocative versions of the thesis.

Although we touched upon it, we have not yet given sufficient atten-tion to the view that television itself constitutes a religion. If this view is sound, then while the distinction between religious television pro-gramming and secular television programming may still be worth pre-serving, on a deeper level of analysis all television programming is to be seen as basically religious, and the experience of those who participate in the communication processes that television involves is to be regarded as a kind of religious experience. According to such a view, television as a form of experience and culture is a variety of religion; even televi-sion as a technology, industry, business, or vocation is better understood when conceived under the category of religion.

Robert Abelman and Stewart M. Hoover provide a comparatively un-pretentious if rather vague articulation of this point of view:

Indeed, there is a sense in which all television is 'religious'. That is, all television seems to be about *meaning*. It is an important conveyor of the social and cultural heritage, and provides its viewers with symbols and ideas which explain pro-found truths about the norms and values of the culture in which they live.[90]

It is hard to know how serious cultural theorists are when they say this sort of thing or how literally they mean us to take their words. To the extent that we accept this point, we are committed to the idea that tele-vision, being religion, is not in competition with religion, although it may be in competition with more traditional forms of religion.

Much depends here on how we are to understand the nature of religion. We have noted that the term *religion* is notoriously ambiguous. Still, it is not so ambiguous that we cannot find fault with a position like the one above. In being "about meaning," and a "conveyor of the social and cultural heritage" or a provider of "symbols and ideas which explain profound truths about the norms and values of the culture," television is no closer to being religion than is a form of experience and culture like philosophy, fine art, history, language, or even science. For that matter, in this sense television is no closer to being religion than it is to being philosophy, art, or language. While it is useful to draw attention to the fact that television is in an important sense a form of culture and experience, not much is to be gained by blurring the significant distinctions between different forms of experience and culture. It is as misleading to characterize television as religion as it would be to characterize philosophy as language, science as philosophy, or history as fine art, although on a certain level of analysis all of these characterizations have some value.

After noting that the view that television constitutes a religion is not uncommonly held, the social psychologist J. Mallory Wober, who associates the position with, among others, such cultural theorists as Michael Novak and Neil Postman,[91] offers counterexamples to the position[92] and in time proceeds to offer an alternative analysis:

A more realistic interpretation of matters is that viewers have psychological and philosophical needs that religions have evolved to meet. Television caters for some of people's needs at these levels, but probably not either in the United States or Great Britain as an exclusive, explicit and established system which can be called a religion by fulfilling the two criteria necessary for this designation (namely, that it shows people the rules of a good life and that it explicitly ascribes authority for these rules to a supernatural entity which is not available for appeal to change or modify the rules). Instead, television mediates the operation of existing established religions, of which there can be only one in any developed society, for example, a denomination of Christendom, or Islam, but not two concomitantly. Television also furthers the functioning of non-established religions and of others which are of long standing and perhaps established in neighboring countries.[93]

Some of this analysis is highly questionable, and Wober's own suggested criteria for the proper application of the term *religion* appear to be rather arbitrary. Nevertheless we can appreciate his point that television caters to only some of the needs that religion has traditionally evolved to meet, and moreover does so in a way that is not as systematic as a natural religion does. He appropriately reminds us of the way in which television "mediates the operation of existing established religions" rather than providing us with a wholly new form of religion. In

Chapters 1 and 2, we acknowledged specific ways in which television has taken on roles that were once primarily played by religion. We also noted, however, the limitations of television as a comprehensive substitute for religion. Rather than reconsidering those limitations, we may simply note here that while television represents a form of experience and culture, it has yet to demonstrate that it is capable of providing people with a worldview that is specific, systematic, and comprehensive in the way that a religious or philosophical worldview is. One would find it difficult if not impossible to explain even in the vaguest terms what one's "commitment" to the "television worldview" involved, whereas even unsophisticated religious believers can usually give us a fairly clear idea of the creed and moral code that lie at the heart of their faith. Of course, when people say that television is a religion, they are often simply making use of hyperbole to indicate what they consider to be the immense cultural importance of television or the great importance that television has come to have in the lives of certain individuals.

According to a related version of the thesis, secular television programming either is "pseudo-religious" or represents religion of an extremely attenuated kind that belongs to a different order than traditional religion. This position, which has affinities with certain religious criticisms of televangelism, fits comfortably with the general view that television is a dangerous rival of genuine religion that is surreptitiously expropriating the major cultural roles traditionally and properly played by religion. William Kuhns, whose orientation is primarily theological, asks,

What if the heroes of films and TV series are in reality the heroes of new myths; and the radio and TV celebrities from Arthur Godfrey to Johnny Carson the high-priests of a new cult? What would be the consequences for people who previously had been sustained on the values and beliefs of a different order? What would be the significance of such a usurpation for Christianity?[94]

He continues:

It is difficult, of course, to locate specifically where religion ends and where the pseudo-religious functions of contemporary society begin. Are man's new myths to be found in the more serious beliefs of scientific and technological progress, or the belief-unbelief fantasies of television westerns and private eye series? The great problem of considering the entertainment media as a pre-emption of religion is that they provide neither transcendence nor the promise of transcendence; and indeed, building on a structure of fantasy and humor, they undermine rather than confirm the traditional modes of belief.[95]

We have already addressed some of these issues, but our concern at this point is whether Kuhns sheds any light on the religious dimension of secular television programming. Kuhns sees important affinities between the heroes, myths, priests, and cults of secular television and those of Christianity; he needs to acknowledge these affinities in order to get his interpretation off the ground. But he then goes on to suggest that in promoting its own heroes, myths, priests, and cults, secular television is usurping roles that properly belong to religion—that television can only offer beliefs and values of a "different order," one intrinsically related to its entertainment functions and, as such, incapable of providing even the promise of transcendence, and that the heroes and myths that it offers are inadequate substitutes for those offered by an authentic religion like Christianity. In giving viewers heroes and myths, secular television is filling some psychological and philosophical needs, but it is cheating the viewers in the process, diverting their attention away from heroes, myths, beliefs, and values that, involving transcendence, could offer them something genuinely spiritual. Thus, there is a "pseudo-religious" dimension to secular television. Although some of its functions have affinities with those of religion, it is incapable of delivering the authentic experience, and worse yet, it discourages people from pursuing authentic religious experience.

Kuhns is impressed by how people use religious terminology to describe secular television's celebrities, shows, and impact; he sees a pattern here.[96] There is indeed a pattern, but I doubt that Kuhns appreciates its importance. Religion is not only an important domain of culture; it is the earliest and most basic form of culture and experience, and all other aspects of "high" culture were built upon it. It is hardly surprising, then, that whether speaking metaphorically, philosophically, or even just carelessly, people should fall back upon religious terminology. Religious terminology is regularly employed in most cultural domains. Long before television was invented, there were "political prophets," "artistic visions," "philosophical cults," "professional bibles," "domestic rites," and so forth. Secular heroes and myths—and beliefs and values—have been conspicuous since ancient times. In fact, the ancients often showed less reverence for religious prophets than for military leaders, statesmen, poets, and athletes, and often they were right to do so.

I certainly share Kuhns' view that the mass media regularly make celebrities out of people who are not entitled to the glorification they receive. In doing so they offer audiences unsatisfactory role models and deflect attention away from the noble, worthy human beings from whom audiences can receive genuine inspiration.[97] Still, we must remember that this criticism could just as well be made by a secularist critic of commercial television programming as by a religious one. Indeed, both secularist and religious critics might justly complain about the surfeit of ecclesiastical celebrities that television parades before us. Again, long before the advent of television, the wrong role models were regularly being thrust before the public eye by promoters of various kinds, including religious zealots, propagandists, proselytizers, and institutional functionaries.

Kuhns attaches great importance to his distinction between the "religious milieu" and television's "entertainment milieu."[98] He states:

The religious milieu depended on fantasies (used as myths) to give greater credibility and solidarity to its primary attempts. Fantasies, essentially, were a tactic, a means. In the entertainment milieu they are their own purpose: they do not really lead to anything, so much as provide short pleasant routes which can (and must) be followed back easily.[99]

Both religion and television are rather more complex in what they have to offer. The entertainment aspect of religion, which was hardly discovered by the televangelists, should not be overlooked, and neither should the serious aspects of television programming, both secular and religious. Moreover, from the standpoint of many high-minded philosophers, the typical religious fantasy is as ludicrous as the typical television fantasy and rather more deleterious in the long run, particularly with respect to what really ought to be the primary attempts of religion. As for transcendence, even if the theologians could reach a consensus on precisely what it involves, it is not as central to spirituality, religious or otherwise, as Kuhns assumes, and some of the world's most profound religious worldviews, most notably in the East, have managed well enough without including it.

Although secular television programming has undoubtedly come to play some of the roles traditionally played by religion, to characterize its performance of those roles as "pseudo-religious" is to poison the wells. The motives of many television programmers, like those of many religious leaders, involve complex aggregates of ideas, attitudes, and ambitions that in some cases are not entirely clear. In being imbued with certain traditional values, attitudes, and metaphysical beliefs, much secular television programming has a significant religious dimension or import. In some of the ways in which it conveys a rich cultural heritage, it mediates the operation of natural religions that have long been institutionalized. Again, however successfully or unsuccessfully it has performed roles previously played by traditional religion, it rarely has pretended or aspired to be a religion as such, and the competition that it has given to established religious institutions in this cultural field has seldom been unfair or underhanded.

Religious critics of television have had a profusion of things to condemn. If they have been sanctimonious at times, they have often been incisive and constructive, especially when they have offered concrete recommendations. Many of their criticisms have not been specifically religious as such, and have also been made by secular critics of television. One does not have to be religious to recognize that too much television programming is sensationalistic, unimaginative, manipulative, and carelessly contrived, and excessively and gratuitously depicts sex and violence, underestimates the intelligence of the average viewer, caters shamelessly to narrow commercial interests, oversimplifies weighty social issues, and promotes unsatisfactory role models. Also, one does not have to be religious to recognize that television programming as a whole does not provide much of a forum to the best and the brightest and virtually ignores entire domains of high culture. Religious critics of television probably believe that their faith commitment obliges them to speak out about the shortcomings of television, but one's incentive to criticize television may stem from a general sense of moral obligation, a sense of civic responsibility, or purely prudential considerations rather than a specifically religious motive.

However, when religious critics of television allude to cultural competition between religion and television, the religious aspect of their criticism is obviously much more significant. One does not have to be religious to appreciate the continuing cultural value of religion or to regret the negative impact of television on traditional religious institutions. It stands to reason, however, that the vast majority of people who will regard this cultural concern as pressing will be people who consider themselves religious, and that the most vocal among these religionists will be those who consider themselves religious leaders. For some observers, the question of the self-interest of religious critics almost spontaneously arises; if the religionists' stake in the matter is not actually vocational, it may nevertheless be personal, existential, and practical. Most people want the dominant forces at work in their culture to accommodate their personal interests and inclinations, even if they are prepared at times to make personal sacrifices for the good of the community. Where an authentic commitment to a worldview is involved, one naturally sees one's personal interests and inclinations as particularly deserving of accommodation.

Those religionists who feel threatened by competition between religion and television may well be sincere when they attack secular television programming for its sensationalism and gratuitous depiction of violence. However, given the importance that they attach to religion, they are likely to regard such failings as symptoms of the real disease, which is the devaluation of religion in their society's cultural life. The key problem in their eyes is creeping secularism. If the tide of secularism could somehow be checked, they will reflect, almost everything else would inevitably fall into place. With regard to television itself, there would be less permissiveness toward commercialism, depictions of violence, and promotion of phony celebrities. The overall quality of communal life would be raised—people would act more compassionately and more responsibly, the crime rate would dramatically decline, there would be fewer unwed mothers, and so forth.

Television, then, is a major target of their criticism because in their view it is a major instrument of the secularization of culture. The basic problem is not that television is undermining their own personal faith—which they tend to regard as steadfast and resolute—but that it is gradually undermining the faith of their fellows, of their society, and in the long run of their progeny.

It may be that whatever the actual intentions of television executives and programmers, the instrument that is largely in their hands is significantly contributing to the secularization of culture. But it is far from evident that television is the primary cause of this secularization, particularly in a pluralistic society that has learned from the mistakes of repressive societies and has gone to great efforts to avoid the kinds of establishment of religion that have resulted in some of the worst assaults on human dignity. It is increasingly fashionable among intellectuals to look down on the naiveté of Enlightenment thinking, but reflective people would generally be more offended than others at having to accommodate their way of life to the arbitrary demands of a despotic majority or elite committed to a worldview very different from their own.

The secularization of culture, in any case, is a complex matter, and making a scapegoat of television may do little to arrest the process. Indeed, in diverting the attention of religionists away from more serious aspects of secularization, it will damage their cause.

In his much discussed theological study *The Secular City*, Harvey Cox made some provocative claims that were especially unsettling for those who regarded themselves as religious conservatives. Cox characterized secularization as,

. . . the loosing of the world from religious and quasi-religious understandings of itself, the dispelling of all closed worldviews, the breaking of all supernatural myths and sacred symbols. It represents "defatalization of history," the discovery of man that he has been left with the world on his hands, that he can no longer blame fortune or the furies for what he does with it. Secularization occurs when a man turns his attention away from worlds beyond and toward this world and this time (*saeculum* = "this present age").[100]

Cox went on to say that,

The forces of secularization have no serious interest in persecuting religion. Secularization simply bypasses and undercuts religion and goes on to other things. It has relativized religious world views and thus rendered them innocuous. Religion has been privatized. It has been accepted as the peculiar prerogative and point of view of a particular person or group. Secularization has accomplished what fire and chain could not: It has convinced the believer that he *could* be wrong, and persuaded the devotee that there are more important things than dying for the faith. The gods of traditional religions live on as private fetishes or the patrons of congenial groups, but they play no significant role in the public life of the secular metropolis.[101]

Perhaps the most striking feature of Cox's analysis was his suggestion that the process of secularization is a consequence of Biblical faith.[102]

Cox's analysis, which now seems somewhat dated, was loaded with gratuitous speculations and generalizations, dubious predictions, and overwrought rhetoric, but he usefully drew the attention of many reflective religionists of the day to the complexity of the secularization process and the strange profundity of some of the attitudes that it had already widely engendered. Even allowing for the flaws in his analysis, how can anyone who understands it take seriously the notion that something like television is largely responsible for the latest phase of the secularization of culture in advanced societies?

There is real competition between religion and television on many levels, but it needs to be kept in perspective. Furthermore, the contribution of religious television, in its more obvious forms and in its secular forms, should not be undervalued. If, in fact, secular television programming represents a field for cooperation between religion and television, that is particularly revealing, not simply because of what it tells us about the relations of religion and television, but because of the hope that it offers to disconsolate students of culture that perhaps in obscure ways the triumph of materialism can be thwarted without Divine intervention.

NOTES TO CHAPTER 3

1. Peter G. Horsfield, *Religious Television: The American Experience* (New York: Longmans, 1984), p. 10.

2. Ibid., p. 8. Cf. pp. 8–10.

3. Ibid., p. 10.

4. Steve Bruce, *Pray TV: Televangelism in America* (London: Routledge, 1990), p. 40.

5. Ibid., p. 41.

6. Jeffery K. Hadden and Charles E. Swann, *Prime Time Preachers: The Rising Power of Televangelism* (Reading, MA: Addison-Wesley, 1981), p. 16.

7. Stewart M. Hoover, *Mass Media Religion: The Social Sources of the Electronic Church* (Newbury Park, CA: Sage Publications, 1988), p. 53.

8. Ibid.

9. Ibid. Cf. also Bruce, *Pray TV*, pp. 31–32.

10. Hadden and Swann, *Prime Time Preachers*, pp. 20–29. Cf. Bruce, *Pray TV*,

pp. 32–36; Michael R. Real, *Mass-Mediated Culture* (Englewood Cliffs, NJ: Prentice-Hall, 1977), ch. 6.

11. Ibid., pp. 32–38. Cf. Bruce, *Pray TV*, pp. 38–39.

12. Ibid., pp. 38–40.

13. Ibid., pp. 40–41.

14. Ibid., pp. 29–32. Cf. Bruce, *Pray TV*, pp. 37–38; Hoover, *Mass Media Religion*, p. 59.

15. Bruce, *Pray TV*, p. 70.

16. Ibid., p. 94.

17. Horsfield, *Religious Television*, p. 161.

18. Hadden and Swann, *Prime Time Preachers*, p. 185.

19. Bruce, *Pray TV*, p. 90.

20. Horsfield, *Religious Television*, p. 39.

21. Quentin J. Schultze, *Televangelism and American Culture: The Business of Popular Religion* (Grand Rapids, MI: Baker Book House, 1991), p. 188.

22. Quentin J. Schultze, *Television: Manna from Hollywood?* (Grand Rapids, MI: Zondervan, 1986), p. 134.

23. Stewart M. Hoover, *The Electronic Giant: A Critique of the Telecommunications Revolution from a Christian Perspective* (Elgin, IL: The Brethren Press, 1982), p. 123.

24. Bruce, *Pray TV*, pp. 77–81.

25. Horsfield, *Religious Television*, p. 126.

26. Hoover, *The Electronic Giant*, p. 123.

27. Horsfield, *Religious Television*, p. 39.

28. Ibid.

29. William James, *The Varieties of Religious Experience* (New York: Longmans, Green, 1902).

30. Plato *Republic* 555B–558C. Cf. 487E–497C.

31. Ibid., 562A–567D.

32. Ibid., 557A–B.

33. Ibid., 499E–500A.

34. Matthew 5:5, 5:7–8, 5:13–14.

35. Bruce, *Pray TV*, p. 90.

36. Ibid., pp. 90–91.

37. Ibid., pp. 81–83.

38. Luke 6:24.

39. Real, *Mass-Mediated Culture*, p. 190.

40. Ibid., p. 201.

41. Bruce, *Pray TV*, p. 94.

42. Ibid., p. 239.

43. Schultze, *Televangelism and American Culture*, pp. 11–12.

44. Ibid., p. 14.

45. Horsfield, *Religious Television*, p. 39.

46. Cf. Hoover, *Mass Media Religion*, p. 235; Bruce, *Pray TV*, pp. 41–48.

47. Jay Newman, *On Religious Freedom* (Ottawa: University of Ottawa Press, 1991), pp. 169–76.

48. Hoover, *Mass Media Religion*, p. 235.

49. Schultze, *Televangelism and American Culture*, p. 188.

50. Ibid.

51. Hoover, *The Electronic Giant*, p. 123.

52. Neil Postman, *Amusing Ourselves to Death: Public Discourse in the Age of Show Business* (New York: Viking, 1985), p. 123.

53. Ibid., p. 122.

54. Razelle Frankl, *Televangelism: The Marketing of Popular Religion* (Carbondale: Southern Illinois University Press, 1987), p. 4.

55. Cf. Newman, *On Religious Freedom*, pp. 24–30, 186–212.

56. John Howard Schütz, *Paul and the Anatomy of Apostolic Authority* (Cambridge: Cambridge University Press, 1975), p. 252. Cf. Newman, *On Religious Freedom*, pp. 197–98.

57. Newman, *On Religious Freedom*, pp. 198–201.

58. Jay Newman, *Competition in Religious Life*, Editions SR, Vol. 11 (Waterloo, ON: Wilfrid Laurier University Press, 1989), pp. 48–64.

59. Matthew 7:1.

60. "In Conversation: Paul Kurtz, International Humanist and Ethical Union," interview by Robert Abelman, in Robert Abelman and Stewart M. Hoover, eds., *Religious Television: Controversies and Conclusions* (Norwood, NJ: Ablex, 1990), p. 154.

61. Cf. Horsfield, *Religious Television*, p. 10.

62. Frankl, *Televangelism*, p. 148.

63. Judith M. Buddenbaum, "Network News Coverage of Religion," in John P. Ferré, ed., *Channels of Belief: Religion and American Commercial Television* (Ames: Iowa State University Press, 1990), p. 76.

64. Cf. Hoover, *Mass Media Religion*, p. 53; Horsfield, *Religious Television*, p. 8.

65. *Great Viewer's Guide* (a bi-monthly publication produced by VISION TV), vol. 5, no. 5 (September and October 1993), p. 2.

66. For a discussion of the historical background, see Dorothy Zolf and Paul W. Taylor, "Redressing the Balance in Canadian Broadcasting: A History of Religious Broadcasting Policy in Canada," *Studies in Religion/Sciences Religieuses*, 18, 2 (1989), pp. 153–70.

67. Cf. Roger Bird, Introduction to Document 9, in Roger Bird, ed., *Documents of Canadian Broadcasting* (Ottawa: Carleton University Press, 1988), p. 37; Report of the Royal Commission, in Bird, *Documents*, p. 53; Board of Broadcast Governors, "Political and Controversial Broadcasting Policies," in Bird, *Documents*, p. 572.

68. *Great Viewer's Guide*, p. 8.

69. Ibid., pp. 26–27.

70. Zolf and Taylor, "Redressing the Balance in Canadian Broadcasting," p. 162.

71. *Great Viewer's Guide*, p. 2.

72. Department of Research and Education of the Federal Council of the Churches of Christ in America, *Broadcasting and the Public: A Case Study of Social Ethics* (New York: Abingdon, 1938), p. 193.

73. Horsfield, *Religious Television*, p. 68.

74. Ibid., p. 180.

75. Robert Sobel, *The Manipulators: America in the Media Age* (Garden City, NY: Anchor Press, 1976), p. 281.

76. Horace Newcomb and Robert S. Alley, *The Producer's Medium: Conversations with Creators of American TV* (New York: Oxford University Press, 1983), p. 72.

77. Ibid., pp. 125–26.

78. J. Brent Bill, *Stay Tuned*, Power Books (Old Tappan, NJ: Fleming H. Revell, 1986), p. 109.

79. Ibid., p. 113.

80. Ibid., pp. 107–8.

81. Ibid., p. 109.

82. Friedrich Nietzsche, *Beyond Good and Evil* (1886), sec. 260, trans. Walter Kaufmann (New York: Vintage Books, 1966), p. 207.

83. Ibid., sec. 265, trans. Kaufmann, p. 215.

84. Howard S. Slusher, *Man, Sport and Existence: A Critical Analysis* (Philadelphia: Lea and Febiger, 1967), p. 136.

85. Ibid., p. 129. Cf. Newman, *Competition in Religious Life*, p. 1.

86. Real, *Mass-Mediated Culture*, pp. 96–103.

87. Ibid., p. 96.

88. Ibid.

89. Cf. Jay Newman, *The Journalist in Plato's Cave* (Rutherford, NJ: Fairleigh Dickinson University Press; London and Toronto: Associated University Presses, 1989), p. 132.

90. Robert Abelman and Stewart M. Hoover, "Introduction" to Abelman and Hoover, ed., *Media Controversies*, p. 4.

91. Wober refers specifically to Postman's *The Disappearance of Childhood* (New York: Delacorte Press, 1982), pp. 108–9. See J. Mallory Wober, *The Use and Abuse of Television: A Social Psychological Analysis of the Changing Screen* (Hillsdale, NJ: Lawrence Erlbaum Associates, 1988), p. 112.

92. Wober, *The Use and Abuse of Television*, p. 113.

93. Ibid., pp. 221–22.

94. William Kuhns, *The Electronic Gospel: Religion and the Media* (New York: Herder and Herder, 1969), p. 9.

95. Ibid., p. 10.

96. Ibid., p. 25.

97. Cf. Jay Newman, *Fanatics and Hypocrites* (Buffalo: Prometheus Books, 1986), pp. 139–42; Newman, *On Religious Freedom*, pp. 197–204, 211.

98. Kuhns, *The Electronic Gospel*, ch. 2.

99. Ibid., pp. 155–56.

100. Harvey Cox, *The Secular City: Secularization and Urbanization in Theological Perspective*, revised ed. (New York: Macmillan, 1966 [1965]), pp. 1–2.

101. Ibid., p. 2.

102. Ibid., p. 15.

CHAPTER FOUR

Competition Between Religion and Television: Competing Forms of Experience and Culture

There is no dearth of important things for social and cultural critics to scrutinize, explain, assess, and deplore, and to endeavor to promote, neutralize, or transform. We therefore should not be surprised that the matter of cultural competition between religion and television is only for a relatively small number of these critics a primary area of concern. Most social and cultural critics will grant that both religion and television are culturally important and influential in various ways, and that there are forms of competition between them that merit close consideration. In defense of their own neglect of the matter, and usually out of conviction as well, they will insist that other matters demand much closer attention from the community of critics. They are right on this point, and whatever conclusions we have reached thus far in our inquiry would seem to support their contention. We have seen that discussions of competition between religion and television have often generated more heat than light, and that this competition is a complex, multifaceted phenomenon that in many of its aspects we may not be in a position to do much about. We have, to be sure, garnered some practical insights along the way, but these could seem trifling in relation to what we have observed about the almost overwhelming complexity of the phenomenon, particularly about the large role played by subjective perspective in making sense of various aspects of the phenomenon.

Even so, we can see that certain aspects of cultural competition between religion and television can be given a direct explanation. Leaders in the fields of religion and television, stimulated by prudential motives and often by higher ones, ordinarily work at maintaining or increasing their cultural influence. For most of them, maintaining and attracting followers is basic to their cultural enterprise. On one level, competition between those active in these two fields is not significantly different from the competition in which they are mutually engaged with people in other fields of culture; thus, for example, whenever people go to a baseball game or to the opera, they are channeling time, money, and interest into a cultural field that might have instead been channeled into the cultural products promoted by leaders in the fields of religion and television. As we have seen, there is much more to cultural competition between religion and television than this, but it is worth our while to remind ourselves that some aspects of this cultural competition are in themselves not complex at all.

However, people who make much of cultural competition between religion and television believe, rightly, that much more is at stake than in most other fields of cultural competition. Religious critics of television, and other critics of television who lament the cultural decline of certain forms of traditional institutional religion, see television as an especially powerful rival of religion. Those active in the field of television, though they may of practical necessity—and often sincerely—declare that they do not think television to be such a rival, have generally been cognizant of the power of religious leaders and religious communities, and have often been fearful and resentful of the efforts of religionists to meddle in their vocational and artistic affairs. They rarely attack religion as such, but in their complaints about direct and indirect forms of censorship, it is often assertive religionists that are implicated as the villainous subverters of freedom, art, creativity, truth, leisure, and joy. When they get very angry at their would-be censors, one can sometimes almost hear them saying, "You self-righteous cranks, let us alone, or we shall take off our gloves and expose you for the nasty peddlers of guilt and hate that you really are."

We have already seen that serious questions can be raised about the actual power of television—and of religion itself—in contemporary Western cultures, and that some of these questions are not easy to answer. Still, religion is, at least from the perspective of history, the most fundamental form of culture, and the one systematic form of experience and culture with which all others have had to reckon sooner or later. And television, unlike baseball or the opera, is not merely a field of culture but a genuine form of experience and culture in its own right. Although it draws on other forms of experience and culture, including religion, for its content, it offers those who appropriate its products a distinctive way of experiencing and communicating about reality by means of symbols. Compared to religion, history, philosophy, science, and fine art, television is in its infancy, but it is much more than just entertainment, industry, or technology. It is a major way of approaching, understanding, and communicating about reality that cannot satisfactorily be subsumed under any of the established categories by which we previously sorted out all human experiences, creations, and appropriations of cultural products. When we penetrate far enough below the surface of their criticisms, we eventually find that it is this quality of television that most troubles the majority of those cultural critics who see television as a powerful agent of secularization and thus a powerful rival of religion. We may think back in this regard to Neil Postman's remark that, "Television is our culture's principal mode of knowing about itself."[1]

The closest that one can come to understanding cultural competition between religion and television "under the aspect of eternity" is to consider them as competing forms of experience and culture in the sense just indicated. What we shall do now is consider competition between religion and television in relation to what was perhaps the most important and most influential cultural competition that ever took place between religion and another form of experience and culture, the ancient competition between religion and philosophy.

Steven Starker, who takes a very negative view of what he characterizes as "crusades against the mass media," usefully compares the situation of those censured in such "crusades" with the situation of the most celebrated of all intellectual martyrs and the greatest human symbol of philosophy itself, Socrates, who was brought to trial by reactionaries in ancient Athens on the charges of impiety and corrupting the youth of Athens with his impious practices. Starker writes:

In the beginning there was the spoken word. Evil influence was simply a matter of listening to the "wrong" people, to bad advice. In ancient Greece, for example, Socrates was condemned to death for his innovative use of the medium of speech. His approach to philosophy and discourse, which encouraged doubt and questioning in all matters, including government and religion, was deemed a corrupting influence upon his youthful students. An "evil influence," Socrates was removed from Greek society by outraged citizens seeking to preserve and protect the values and morals of their culture and children.[2]

It may initially seem strange to find leaders in the field of television, and the mass media generally, represented as heirs of the greatest secular saint of the ancient world, a man of immense integrity who made remarkable personal sacrifices so that his fellow human beings could come to appreciate the value of reason in the cultivation and promotion of virtue. Few people actively involved in the production of television programs approach saintliness, are prepared to make great personal sacrifices, or are chiefly committed to the promotion of reason and virtue. Still, it is apposite to recall that in his own time, Socrates, this great human symbol of the spirit of philosophical reflection, was far from being universally regarded as a saint, and indeed was the victim of intense vilification by reactionary religionists who saw him—and the philosophical concerns that he promoted and came to represent—as subverting the religious foundations of his society's traditional culture. Socrates received "good press" from his devoted student, Plato, who in his extremely influential writings generally portrays Socrates not only as a deeply religious person but as the restorer of his troubled society's lost spirituality.[3] Countless generations of academic humanists and other promoters of reason and enlightenment have kept this Platonic image of Socrates alive in the minds of those who would be wiser and better human beings. But as Plato himself knew, entrenched authoritarian elites, in religion as well as in politics, education, the fine arts, and other cultural domains, generally have good reason to feel threatened by the Socratic enterprise, with its emphases on intellectual freedom, responsibility, and rigor, and on the existential, moral, social, and cultural importance of overcoming irrational superstition, emotionalism, conventionalism, tribalism, traditionalism, and blind faith. Although he bitterly resented the characterization of Socrates by his detractors as a dangerous antireligious Sophist, Plato was himself worried about the consequences of disrespect for established religious authority.[4]

In his analysis of the unfairness of Socrates' detractors, Plato singles out the comic poet, Aristophanes, for special mention,[5] for in his influential play, the *Clouds*, Aristophanes, though a friend of Socrates, provides an especially vivid image of Socrates, or the philosophical spirit that Socrates represents, as a subverter of traditional religion and its central role in culture. At the end of this caustic comedy, the protagonist, burning down the school of Socrates, censures him and his disciples with these extremely severe words: "You have insulted all the blessed Gods in Heaven / and peered into the crevices of the Lady Moon! / Strike, don't spare a single one of them, they deserve it, / especially because they have blasphemed the Gods!"[6] It is not always easy to conceive of Aristophanes, the writer of hilariously bawdy plays, as a defender of religious orthodoxy, and much of the *Clouds* is simply a matter of a professional satirist poking fun at a convenient target. Still, Aristophanes was undoubtedly worried about the cultural consequences of all of this big questioning, reasoning, and independent thinking that Socrates was encouraging, particularly among the brightest young people of Athens. Aristophanes' criticism of Socrates and his philosophy was to be echoed later not only by those who had Socrates brought to trial but by many generations of religious critics of philosophy. To this day, there are still many influential religious thinkers, functionaries, preachers, and teachers who are troubled by what they perceive as the major role played by philosophy in engendering antireligious tendencies such as skepticism, secularism, and disrespect for religious authority.

In our own society, we often take rationality for granted, even though we know that all of us are at least sometimes irrational. But before the age of the greatest philosophers of ancient Greece, the concept of rationality itself was not at all clear. It was only when the classical Greek philosophers began to promote their distinctive notion of *logos* that our modern conception of rationality started to take shape. Once the ancient Greek philosophers started promoting their inquiries, all aspects of Western culture, including religion itself, began to be significantly transformed. Religion survived the rise of philosophy, and indeed throughout history has in many ways been enriched by philosophy's influence upon it, but it has changed in large part because of the need of religious leaders to respond to the demands of the promoters of reason and their followers. Although they rarely attacked religion as such, the earliest philosophers initiated the rational liberalization of religion, and every generation of philosophers has contributed to the extension and advancement of this process.[7] Philosophers have only rarely regarded themselves as direct competitors of religious thinkers, functionaries, preachers, and teachers—and have often played some of these roles—but they recognized from the start that they were involved in an immensely important cultural competition with the representatives and promoters of a traditional illiberal religion that does not make proper allowance for human rationality and its fundamental importance for personal, social, and cultural development. Reactionary religious leaders resisted the incursion of the earliest promoters of philosophical reason into their affairs, and throughout history, there have been periods when reactionary religious sentiment has led to the temporary but significant restoration of illiberal, anti-intellectual religio-cultural patterns; and, of course, there are reactionary religious leaders, sometimes very gifted ones, in every society. However, if one takes a wide view of the history of Western culture, one can see that the leading representatives of religion as a form of experience and culture have with an impressive regularity recognized the practical necessity of entering into a *modus vivendi* with the representatives of almost every new worldview promoted by nearly every major movement in the history of philosophy.

When one looks at our own society, and modern Western societies in general, one may be led to conclude that in the ancient and continuing cultural competition between religion and philosophy, religion has for all intents and purposes won out. Philosophy has survived, and has a certain respectability in most higher educational circles, even in those that emphasize the fundamental cultural importance of traditional religious symbols, values, and orientations. Still, on a certain level, religion was destined to be victorious, because philosophy could never be a mass phenomenon. With its focus on abstract concepts and its demands for logical rigor and familiarity with an ever-increasing body of esoteric literature and terminology, it is not appealing to the masses. In contrast, religion, while it offers its followers opportunities for deep reflection, including philosophical reflection, appeals to all sorts of people with widely varying intellectual capabilities and inclinations. For those who are uncomfortable with its more profound aspects, it still can provide personally desired (and socially desirable) forms of security, order, direction, hope, and encouragement by means of its rites, mysteries, myths, spectacles, and talk about miracles and salvation. Berdyaev's wise observation comes to mind:

The masses participate in culture. That is both right and necessary: the masses must not remain in darkness. In the past the masses participated in culture by way of religion, and the culture of the broad masses was almost exclusively a religious culture. Religion was the meeting-place of the masses with the aristocratic cultural class. Only religion is capable of making such a combination: neither philosophy nor science, nor enlightenment, nor art nor literature can do this. Deprived of religious basis, any high-qualitative culture inevitably becomes separated from popular life and an isolated cultural elite is produced, which keenly feels its uselessness to the people.[8]

To appreciate fully religion's inevitable "victory" over philosophy, we must consider another factor. Philosophy is the "child" of religion. Although philosophy provides people with a distinctive form of experience and culture, one that offers them rational worldviews, even in its most positivistic and naturalistic varieties it carries with it a legacy that it has inherited from religion, and this legacy can never be wholly negated. The classical scholar, F. M. Cornford, has observed that,

There is a real continuity between the earliest rational speculation and the religious representation that lay behind it; and this is no mere matter of superficial analogies, such as the allegorical equation of the elements with the Gods of popular belief. Philosophy inherited from religion certain great conceptions—for instance, the ideas of "God," "Soul," "Destiny," "Law"—which continued to circumscribe the movements of rational thought and to determine their main directions. Religion expresses itself in poetical symbols and in terms of mythical personalities; philosophy prefers the language of dry abstraction, and speaks of *substance, cause, matter,* and so forth. But the outward difference only disguises an inward and substantial affinity between these two successive products of the same consciousness. The modes of thought that attain to clear definition and explicit statement in philosophy were already implicit in the unreasoned intuitions of mythology.[9]

No matter how hard some have tried, philosophers have never been able to cut philosophy off completely from its religious roots. When they have tried, what they have ended up with is something that hardly qualifies as philosophy according to our historical understanding of it. Philosophy could never have emerged as a new and distinctive form of experience and culture, as a new way of viewing the world, if those involved in its development had declined to enter into a vigorous cultural competition with reactionary religious forces. Nevertheless, its dependence on a certain amount of pre-rational religious material is permanently fixed. As philosophy's own "child," science, has developed, some philosophers have tried to make philosophy more scientific, but most philosophers and most cultural theorists have come to regard the special kinship between philosophy and religion as all the more obvious. On this level, religion cannot lose; it provides the basic program of philosophy, and the work of philosophy represents the elucidation and clarification of religious material, or of pre-religious material that has been mediated to philosophy via religious experience and culture.[10]

Yet on another level the Child is father of the Man. When the earliest philosophers set their followers to thinking in a rational way, it was inevitable that people's understanding of religion, and ultimately religion itself, would be comprehensively transformed. No sane person sacrifices animals to the gods in New York, Toronto, or Athens, and in these places, it is not easy to find people who believe in the gods. Furthermore, if certain philosophers, theologians, and behavioral and social scientists are right, the God in whom so many people now profess to believe is very different from the God in whom their "fathers" believed. No less than Aristophanes and Socrates, the prophet Elijah and the apostle Paul would be astounded by what they read in the writings of most theologians on the faculties of the major universities of the modern world. When, in their characteristic manner, they went out to confront real sinners in the real world, particularly those who profess to be true believers, they would be all the more astounded.

The rational liberalization of religion, which philosophy initiated and has carried on for over two thousand years, has played an enormous part in the advancement of civilization, but if philosophy has been a good "child" and sustained and enriched religion, it has also taken much away from religion in the process. Thoughtful religionists often sense that; they may understand that the rational liberalization of religion, whatever good it has accomplished, has led to a certain dilution of religious commitment.[11] Wise religionists will not gloat when they reflect on the general neglect of philosophy by the masses who remain religious in at least an attenuated form; nor will they gain much consolation from reflection on how television programming, for example, pays a hundred times more attention to religion and religionists than it does to philosophy and philosophers. For they will understand not only that the neglect of philosophy is one more evidence of the decline of spirituality and the growth of materialism, but that the powerful influence of philosophy is still to be encountered whenever and wherever people who are not in awe of God and His earthly agents are going about their business in a "rational" way. Such people may still consider themselves religious, and may indeed be religious; and they may never have read a single paragraph of philosophical literature, or even arrived at a clear conception of what philosophy is. Nonetheless, in their own way they are to be counted among the heirs to the Socratic tradition.

Nietzsche, himself a philosopher and, moreover, no friend of God, priests, reactionaries, or traditional religion, has, oddly enough, provided one of the most eloquent descriptions of the price that we moderns may be paying for the triumph of Socratism over its cultural competitors:

Here we have our present age, the result of a Socratism bent on the extermination of myth. Man today, stripped of myth, stands famished among all his pasts and must dig frantically for roots, be it among the most remote antiquities. What does our great historical hunger signify, our clutching about us of countless other cultures, our consuming desire for knowledge, if not the loss of myth, of a mythic home, the mythic womb?[12]

But the triumph of Socratism, either over traditional religion or over materialism, is far from complete. For the reasons that we have considered, its triumph over traditional religion could never be complete. Religion and philosophy continue to interact in many complex ways, some competitive and some not, and their relations have been further complicated by their interaction with science, particularly in recent years with the behavioral and social sciences.[13]

The question now before us is what is to be learned about cultural competition between religion and television from relevant features of the historic cultural competition between religion and philosophy. Philosophy and television are, to be sure, very different phenomena, and in many ways it is impossible to conceive of them as belonging to the same order of phenomena. Yet if we can understand them as forms of experience and culture, then we should be able to appreciate certain things that they have in common as cultural rivals of religion. Moreover, we may find that even certain differences between them can be illuminating.

Retracing our steps, we return to the observation that the spirit in which television and other mass media are attacked by many who seek, in Starker's words, "to preserve and protect the values and morals of their culture and their children," is not entirely unlike the spirit in which Socrates was attacked by religious reactionaries in ancient Athens for his approach to philosophy. Let us consider this matter more closely. If we may trust Plato's account, then Socrates himself was aware of the fact that although his reactionary critics professed to be troubled by the content of his teaching, it was actually something quite different about his activity, which may not even have been "teaching" at all,[14] that really troubled them, although they were not clear on this point.[15] Socrates, who unlike Plato and other later philosophers constantly professed his own ignorance and had no doctrines to teach, was a man of questions, and by asking questions to authorities in public places, and showing observers that the answers given by these authorities could not withstand rational critical analysis, he encouraged the observers to reflect for themselves, in a disciplined rational manner, on the important value issues that had been raised. He did not offer these observers new ideas—although it was almost inevitable that his disciples would—but offered them a way of understanding things, the way of reason or rationality, that would free them from their dependence on supposed cultural authorities. Unable to meet Socrates' demand for a rational response to his questions, the entrenched authoritarian elites of his society concluded that there was something subversive about what Socrates was doing, and at a loss to explain precisely what that was, they attributed to him heterodox doctrines that in fact he did not hold.[16] Socrates was indeed subverting their personal influence; he exposed their ignorance in public. But it was not any doctrines that Socrates was teaching that subverted their influence. Rather, it was the access that Socrates was giving observers to a new way of understanding things, one partly independent of cultural tradition and convention, that was resulting in their loss of prestige. Disposing of Socrates did not do the reactionaries any good. As Socrates prophesied, once people get the hang of this "rational inquiry," and appreciate its full value in promoting personal, social, and cultural development, force and deception will not be enough to stop them from carrying on with it, in public as well as in private life.[17] The reactionaries were doomed in the long run. Philosophy did not simply offer a rival set of beliefs or values, but rather it offered a new way of seeing and doing things, a rational way.

Few people actively involved in television programming are as high-minded as Socrates, yet reactionary criticism of television is in some ways reminiscent of ancient criticism of Socrates and his philosophy. Television programming, of course, does have content, and critics of television are often right to criticize the content of specific television programs and specific types of television programming. However, in their criticism of television and television programming, reactionary critics who do not fully comprehend the nature of the phenomena frequently misrepresent the content of most television programming. Seeking to uncover hidden messages being directed at a gullible, manipulable audience by a devious cabal, they erroneously attribute doctrines to television programmers in much the same way Socrates' reactionary critics erroneously attributed heterodox doctrines to him. Like Socrates' critics, these modern critics fail to realize that television's cultural competition with established cultural institutions is not primarily on the level of beliefs and values or any form of content as such, but rather a matter of the new forms of perception and understanding that television makes possible. They naively assume, in Marshall McLuhan's words, that, "If the TV tube fires the right ammunition at the right people it is good."[18] But program and content analysis offer few clues to the magic or subliminal charge of television,[19] or its influence in translating experience into new forms and enabling people to let go of their environment in order to grasp it in a new way.[20]

Television undoubtedly can be subversive to authoritarian elites, but when it is, it is normally not so much because of the rival propaganda it disseminates as because of the stimulus to reflection it offers by means of the new perspective it provides. Television is not merely a means of communication; it offers us an access to reality that human beings previously did not have. Consider this simple, straightforward example. Television brings the horrors of war into the living rooms of people sitting in their sofas or armchairs in another part of the globe. The people responsible for transmitting the images of the struggle can select and manipulate those images in numerous ways, and with antiauthoritarian motives, proauthoritarian motives, or independent motives. But while the motives of those responsible for the transmission of the images are undeniably worthy of consideration, the power of television to provide us with access to realities that were previously unavailable to us in this direct form is, in itself, at least as important. Manipulated though it may be, this coverage makes people sensitive to concrete evils in the world in a way that neither religion nor philosophy, history nor testimony, belles lettres nor print journalism can. When one sees living, breathing, talking human beings bloodied and mutilated, perhaps because of policies pursued by our government or its allies, constructive moral criticism is naturally evoked.[21] Even if no effort were being made to manipulate viewers with these images for self-serving or ideological purposes, what we would be seeing on the television screen would still represent a distortion of reality. People in the war zone are, among other things, not just two-dimensional and three inches tall. When we view these atrocities, we are not literally "on the scene" in the way that the soldiers and war correspondents are, and we are deceived if we believe that we are. But the distortion involved in such coverage is not necessarily any more dangerous or misleading than that involved in a religious sermon, a philosophical argument, an historical account, or a literary representation. We should remember in this regard that religionists, philosophers, historians, belletrists, and print journalists have also been known to have any number of antiauthoritarian, proauthoritarian, or independent motives.

My simple example barely scratches the surface. When, for example,

McLuhan explored the ways in which television has "changed our sense-lives and our mental processes,"[22] he drew attention to such things as its rejection of the sharp personality,[23] its involvement in depth in a situation,[24] and its "low definition" image.[25] And he argued further that the way in which we perceive television images carries over to our perception in everyday life.[26] Although most of his claims about television and perception have been challenged, they have been, at very least, usefully suggestive and provocative.

We may reasonably expect most cultural theorists to resist efforts to compare television with philosophy as forms of experience and culture, even simply with respect to their competitive relationship with religion. Such resistance can be explained on several levels. First, television is, relative to philosophy and its characteristic forms of rational understanding, extremely new. Its psychological, behavioral, and social consequences are not yet much understood from a humanistic perspective, and even empirical behavioral and social-scientific approaches to explaining them have yet to yield much upon which cultural theorists can agree. McLuhan, though he focused on television as a medium or technology, was helpful in pointing to and explaining the conservative bias of most cultural elites (as well as the general public) in their assessment of the cultural importance of any new medium, particularly with respect to its role in changing perception.[27] Because television is so new, it has yet to provide a sufficient amount of classic material to qualify as a full-fledged cultural discipline in the eyes of those responsible in universities and elsewhere for determining what qualifies as high culture. A related point is that the production of television's cultural products is habitually associated by most serious cultural observers more with business and industrial motives than with any properly creative or cultural motives. While this is understandable to some extent, the narrower, self-serving motives of many involved in the production and promotion of religious, philosophical, scientific, and artistic cultural products should not be ignored. Here again it will be useful to consider the rise of philosophy.

It is easy enough now to contrast the noble Socrates with the influential types in the television industry who are preoccupied with the economic "bottom line." And let us grant for the sake of argument that the cultural idealism of even the best and brightest people involved in television programming generally falls short of that which has inspired the typical philosopher (or religious functionary, scientist, or belletrist). Still, the fact remains that Plato himself recognized the need to go to great efforts to explain to his fellow citizens why Socrates was not just one more manipulative, self-serving Sophist like Callicles or Thrasymachus. By the time Socrates appeared on the scene in Athenian life, decent folk had good reason to be suspicious of smooth-talking rhetoricians who saw their sophisticated reasoning as a way of becoming rich, famous, and powerful. Even the noblest of these Sophists, such as Protagoras, carried on their vocation of moral teaching as a business, and in advertising their services, they let potential students and clients know that being more rational than the ignorant masses was lucrative as well as civilizing. The Sophists were widely mistrusted not only because they were foreigners, or because they promoted culturally threatening varieties of subjectivism, relativism, and religious skepticism, but because they were all too often little more than venal, manipulative "operators." The earlier pre-Socratic philosophers had generally eschewed controversial moral and political theorizing; Socrates, both in his emphasis on virtue and in his philosophical method, was in important ways the heir to the Sophistic tradition that he and Plato detested. In attacking the Sophists, and distancing Socrates and himself from their narrower motives and extreme ethical and theological positions, Plato essentially acknowledged that the most conspicuous representatives and promoters of reason in his society were indeed corrupt and dangerous subversives.[28] Although it suited Plato's purposes to dismiss the Sophists as pseudo-philosophers, his own promotion of reason in harmony with virtue, and the Socratic enterprise from which it was born, would not have been possible without the revolutionary accomplishments of these somewhat shady predecessors. We see, then, that even the emergence of philosophy as an autonomous form of experience and culture, and of the modern conception of rationality, involved the extraordinary productive activity of certain individuals whose personal integrity and cultural idealism fell far short of Socrates'.[29]

The people who invented television as a technology were not ignoramuses. Quite to the contrary, they were generally highly educated applied scientists. Some of them may be regarded as having been brilliantly creative. If they were, by inclination and vocation, more scientific than humanistic, it hardly follows that they were amoral technocrats. They put their technological skills and imagination at the service not only of businessmen or manipulative cultural elites but of their fellow citizens, their society, and humanity. They were generally intelligent enough to understand that the basic product that they were creating, in bringing a new kind of visual image into the lives of their fellow human beings, conceivably had enormous cultural (and anticultural) potential. They must also have realized that although their research and product development required them to enter into contracts with businessmen and bureaucrats who were less than idealistic, the uses to which the new technology would be put would, in the long run, be determined not only by manipulative, self-serving "operators," but by the general public and by progressive, enlightened cultural forces. The imaginative conception of the technology itself would not have been possible if the inventors of television had not themselves been heirs to a very old cultural tradition that was born from language and religion and involved the successive development of such forms of experience and culture as philosophy, science, and art. Still, they were not seers who could predict precisely how in the course of time the new technology would develop, be used, and be misused. The businessmen and bureaucrats were not seers either; neither were the first people involved in television programming nor the earliest defenders and critics of the new medium. In this sense, television, like all media—and like all forms of experience and culture—was "put out" before it was "thought out."[30]

Although television has already offered us a new form of perception, it is still the "child" of the multifaceted culture out of which it has grown. It is directly the child of science and technology, and no less importantly, it is indirectly, in its fundamental conception as well as in its actual programming, the child—or distant descendant—of religion, philosophy, and art. To be sure, it has already transformed our conceptions of religion and rationality in important ways. On a certain level, it is in competition with long-established forms of experience and culture, and the promoters of those forms of experience and culture will increasingly recognize the practical necessity of entering into a *modus vivendi* with television in its ensuing phases of technological and programming development. Still, it has no more been the intention of most leaders in the field of television to destroy religion than it has been the intention of most philosophers to destroy religion. It would, of course, be folly to endeavor to do such a thing.

Like philosophy, television has in its own way contributed to the liberalization of religion. Limited though their cultural idealism may be, most people responsible for television programming believe in the positive cultural value that television affords the viewer. Though they may be embarrassed by the content of particular television programs, there is usually little if any cant in their affirmation that television, properly employed, reveals important truths and realities to the viewer that could not otherwise be apprehended, or at least could only be apprehended with very great effort and good fortune. On this level television people are genuinely liberal; they want viewers to have access to dimensions of truth and reality that have hitherto remained hidden from them. Religious critics of television are undoubtedly right when they say that television often presents a distorted picture of traditional religion. But in presenting religion as it does, particularly when it is not being manipulative, television programming enables us to see and understand religious phenomena in a new and useful light. When religious and other cultural critics attack television for having deprived religion of its profoundly spiritual, mystical, awesome dimensions, their complaint can be understood on many levels, but in one sense it echoes Nietzsche's complaint that philosophy, Socratism, stripped traditional culture of its nourishing myths. As we have seen, philosophy from the start led to a certain dilution of religious commitment, but it did much good in the process by freeing people from irrational superstition, emotionalism, and tribalism, and by providing them with conditions of an existential commitment richer in its own way than the form of commitment it had weakened. Television, with or without the aid of reason, regularly exposes the weaknesses of traditional illiberal religion. It helps us to see how much "smaller" religious authorities are than they would have had our ancestors believe; it shows us the pathetic, helpless victims of age-old religious wars and of the economic, psychological, and sexual exploitation of ecclesiastical functionaries. It enables us to see, by viewing them from a distance, how silly religious rites can be and how they are often used to obscure the ethical teachings of great prophets. It exposes hatemongers, hucksters, and hypocrites, being the most effective at this when it leaves them free to expose themselves. Also, it offers us a glimpse into the ways of people of other faiths, and enables us to see that these people are not necessarily shallow and stupid. It enables us to participate, if only from a great distance, in a genuinely pluralistic religious community, and it encourages us to consider religion as one of many socio-cultural fields, alongside such secular ones as politics, business, labor, sport, and medicine. Of course, television has often been exploited by religious, political, and other reactionaries—as have philosophy and reason—but there is nothing special about it in that regard. Reactionary causes have been served by philosophers and theologians, poets and scientists, artists and artisans.

Unlike philosophy, television is a mass phenomenon. It appeals to the masses. It does not demand, as philosophy does, ability to grasp complex abstract concepts, logical rigor, and familiarity with a body of esoteric literature and terminology. It does not even demand much in the way of rationality. Normally, it only requires the ability to manipulate a few simple controls: one that turns the machine on and off, one that controls volume, and one that changes channels. Undoubtedly, its mass appeal is to be explained in part by the limited demands that it makes of the unsophisticated, intellectually limited viewer. Nonetheless, its being uncomplicated does not alone explain its mass appeal. It is appealing in large part because it offers something concrete, and it offers different programs for different viewer types. As religion traditionally has done, television enables the masses to participate in culture; it offers something to people of widely varying intellectual capabilities and inclinations. However, those critics who see television as reducing everything to entertainment, or avoiding all exposition and attempting never to induce perplexity,[31] fail to recognize that television, like religion, generally offers something to reflective types as well as backward and immature types, and that at times it serves well, as religion traditionally did, as the meeting-place of the masses with the aristocratic cultural class.

The mass appeal of television understandably makes religious traditionalists edgy in a way that the influence of philosophy no longer does.
Reactionary religionists are still worried about the influence of icono-
clastic intellectuals in universities and elsewhere, and more sophisticated
religious traditionalists are still regularly given to reflection on the complex interaction between those who emphasize faith and those who emphasize reason. Thoughtful religious cultural theorists realize that
philosophy not only survives among small cultural elites but also manifests itself in all circumstances in which people are trying to be reasonable about matters of great cultural importance. They can see that despite
whatever *modus vivendi* is in place, the tensions between traditional religion and the spirit of philosophy can never be fully resolved. But the
mass appeal of television—or of the new forms of technology that are
growing out of it—is more threatening. That is because, first, television
encroaches upon nonrational domains of personal, social, and cultural
development that philosophy has in the past had to leave to religion. It
is there not only for the simple and the intellectually torpid but for the
very young child who has yet to reach the stage of development at which
she can grasp even rudimentary logical conceptions. Where Socratism
turns its back on myth, emotion, spectacle, and tribal consciousness, television routinely steps in, impressively performing roles that philosophy
by its very nature was historically forced to leave to the form of experience and culture from which it had descended. The philosophically
inclined will thus appreciate the exquisite irony involved in the complaint of some religious critics of television that television promotes ir-
rationality.

Moreover, there is a certain universality to many forms of television
programming that neither traditional religion nor philosophy has ever
enjoyed. Religion has never been able to transcend completely its tribal
aspect. Religious critics of television are right to say that in its handling
of religion, television has not been able to offer everything that is provided by active participation in a religious community. However, mem-
bership in a religious community involves distancing oneself in
important ways from members of other religious communities or secular
communities. The result can be forms of estrangement and conflict that
are not entirely salutary for individuals, communities, or humanity as a
whole. Some thinkers of the Age of Reason and the Enlightenment saw
philosophy as capable of generating a universal rational faith, but the
squabbling among philosophical schools, sects, and cults has always
been a salient feature of intellectual life. Television, of course, can appeal
to and reinforce tribal loyalties, and on a certain level a television program is necessarily as culture-bound as any other cultural product. But
in some of its forms, television programming tends to "travel" better
than religion or philosophy, as is most impressively manifested in the

ability of particular forms of television programming to appeal to people
of very different communities with very different faiths and worldviews.
The comparativist must often do massive spadework to uncover the ar-
chetypes underlying world religions and philosophies. Often his or her
critics will complain that so little has been dug up that the effort was
largely wasted. Yet cartoon shows, variety shows, dramatic shows, and
even many news shows regularly appeal alike to religionists and secularists, Europeans and Asians, simpletons and intellectuals, children and
adults, women and men. It is often hard to conceive of religion apart
from religions or of philosophy apart from philosophies. In contrast, the
distinctive global outreach of certain forms of television programming
enables television simultaneously to promote a universal culture and to
make cultural diversity more agreeable. This is not entirely a good thing,
but if religious traditionalists feel threatened by it, that, I suggest, is not
simply because of the ways in which it is a bad thing. Religious traditionalists may be prompted by, say, bigotry or a pathological fear of
change, to take a dim view of television's influence in this regard.

Finally, television frightens some religionists, both liberal and illiberal
ones, for one of the reasons that it also frightens some philosophers and
some secular cultural theorists and critics. It represents the unknown; it
is still relatively new, it is rapidly evolving, and it is contributing to the
birth and growth of new media, new technologies, and potentially even
new forms of experience and culture that we have not yet been able to
conceive. For some, it inspires a terror comparable to that which Socratism inspired when it first appeared in Aristophanes' world. Unfortunately, terror rarely gives way to a thoughtful, responsible, measured,
and constructive response to evils, real or imagined.

When religion and television are regarded as competing forms of experience and culture, a golden opportunity is presented for disengage-
ment from the hollow, unproductive carping and recrimination that so
often vitiate cultural criticism of television. That is because one will be
better positioned to see beyond matters of "venality," "conspiracy," and
"unfairness" and to confront the essential matter of culture itself. From
this new vantage point one may initially be struck by a disquieting irony.
Although religion and television are ultimately rooted in human nature
and nature generally, they are not merely natural phenomena to be understood through the cognitive methods of natural science. Rather, they
are cultural products precisely because they represent the conscious efforts of human beings to make use of their distinctively human capacities
to meliorate the condition of their fellows. Yet while they are human
creations, these cultural products can take on a life of their own and can
exert a determining influence on human thought and action that is as
rigid, compelling, and difficult to comprehend as some of the most intractable forces of nature. If one dwells on this irony too long, the result

will be a paralyzing determinism that is even less productive than any carping and recrimination. Thus, those who would contribute to the advancement of culture and civilization have an obligation to understand that to some extent, "Humankind has the freedom, on the one hand, to appreciate what is freeing and, on the other hand, to change what is not."[32] Religion itself can be either a hindrance or a help in this regard. When it emphasizes the smallness of human beings in relation to higher forces, it can be a powerful disincentive to cultural creativity;[33] but when it emphasizes the dignity and responsibility of human beings who truly matter in the cosmic order, it can be an incomparable inspiration to cultural creativity.[34]

Much that has been said in this study can fairly be construed as a defense of television from dogmatic, self-serving, frivolous, or misguided forms of religious and "para-religious" criticism. We have nonetheless established that there is a genuine competition between religion and television and that those who believe in the irreplaceable cultural value of the kind of religion to which they are committed have an interest in protecting it from threats to its integrity that television poses. To the extent that religion is a matter of faith or a basic worldview, it is something that generates or legitimates its own standards of truth, reality, and goodness. But a thoughtful, high-minded religionist in a pluralistic society understands that there is a need to enter into dialogue and cooperation with other thoughtful, high-minded individuals who, though they do not share the same faith, are just as committed to the cultural advancement of the society. Despite its limitations, reason can help one to participate constructively in such dialogue and cooperation. Although the tensions between faith and reason should not be ignored, the woman or man of faith should be reluctant to embrace such alternatives to reason as force and deception.

While there is genuine competition between religion and television, it behooves religious critics of television to remember that much that they abhor about television is also odious not only to people of other religious faiths but to reflective individuals who do not regard themselves as religious. In a pluralistic society, it is prudent as well as moral to articulate criticisms of television, when possible, in terms that such people can understand and appreciate; if no effort is made to do this, the critic will likely appear to be a bigot, and the common cause will be undermined.

Religion is the prototypical form of culture, and one cannot fully understand modern culture without understanding and appreciating its religious sources. However, we have reached a stage in the development of culture and civilization at which it is appropriate to distinguish conceptually between religion and culture; while we may still regard religion as the essence of culture, we can also see that in another way it is one of many forms and aspects of culture. Even the most devout religionist does not always see things "religiously." If that was once possible, it certainly no longer is.

Not only is much that high-minded religionists deplore about television also deplored by reflective secular moralists, but thoughtful people in the television field will themselves grant that television has had an anticultural impact by contributing in certain ways to the decline of literacy, the promotion of shallow celebrities as role models, the spread of materialistic values and attitudes, and the institutionalization of passivity. They may well add that television has also promoted literacy, held up estimable role models, exposed people to spiritual values and attitudes, and stimulated people to act. They could further add that inauthentic cultural products were put forward by self-serving manipulators and operators in religion and other domains long before the invention of television, and are still being put forward by venal types in those domains. In any case, those concerned with the advancement of culture and civilization need to continue to encourage people in the television field to work harder to minimize the anticultural impact of their programming. They are likely to be more successful in performing this role if they indicate to those in the television field that they regard them not as sinners in need of redemption but rather as emerging craftspeople who can do the best for themselves and for their fellows if they remain sensitive to the constructive criticism and advice of intelligent, knowledgeable, and compassionate representatives of long-established forms of experience and culture.

Although cultural products can take on a life of their own apart from the conceptions and intentions of their human creators, adapters, and promoters, it is their having been created by human beings with specific intentions that makes them cultural products rather than simply natural phenomena. Long before the emergence of philosophical reason, human beings were capable of conceiving moral and other evaluative criteria and aspiring to meliorate their own condition and that of their family members and fellow tribesmen. We cannot know to what extent this mode of thinking gave rise to religion and to what extent it developed from religion, but once human beings were capable of it, cultural processes were then possible, and human activity took on a new order of meaning. Despite the influence of positivistic social science, the term *culture* has never been completely divorced from its original association with cultivation and nurture, and the idea of culture was firmly fixed in people's minds long before this name for it was coined. In assessing cultural activity, human beings from the start considered both how cultural products make people better and how they make people better off. It would appear, however, that they were not very clear about the relation or the relative importance of these two forms of melioration. Even today, there are divergent opinions on such matters. Still, even before the rise of philosophy, people made discriminating judgments, and often sophisticated ones, about what products are genuinely meliorative and what products are being deceptively passed off as such by people with questionable motives.

When religious and other cultural critics of television pass a negative judgment on television programming, they usually are not merely disapproving of the consequences of such programming, but are calling into question the motivation of those responsible for the creation and promotion of the programming. They are troubled not only by the anti-cultural impact of the programming—its failure to be genuinely meliorative—but by what they perceive as the less-than-noble spirit in which the programming has been conceived. They see too many people highly placed in the television field as insufficiently concerned with the more important forms of cultural melioration, and they see many of these people as prepared to put forward products that are, on balance, not genuinely meliorative at all. Their criteria of what constitutes the genuinely meliorative may be rather arbitrary and dogmatic, but they may still be serving the community well by encouraging people in the television field to take a hard look at their values and ambitions and to provide their fellows with concrete evidence of their commitment to cultural melioration.

However, when cultural critics of television insist that the forces of television are in competition with the forces of culture that they themselves represent, it is wholly appropriate for an open-minded observer to raise questions not only about their criteria for regarding products as genuinely meliorative but about how earnest and how successful these promoters of "culture" have been. Some of these questions pose a special problem for the religious critic of television, at least the Christian or Jewish one, for although such a person should be a witness for his or her faith, he or she must be ever mindful of the need for humility. "The fear of the Lord *is* the instruction of wisdom; and before honor *is* humility."[35] "He hath shown thee, O man, what *is* good; and what doth the Lord require of thee, but to do justly, and to love mercy, and to walk humbly with thy God?"[36] For a Christian or Jew to be righteous, indignation must be tempered by honest self-criticism as well as charity even for cultural rivals. The arrogance that marks much religious criticism of television is unbecoming, as is, more importantly, the failure of many religious critics of television to get their own house in order. If television has deprived religious leaders of some of the glory and authority to which their predecessors were accustomed, perhaps that is not such a bad thing for them. "Though the Lord *be* high, yet hath he respect unto the lowly: but the proud he knoweth afar off."[37]

We have taken note of television's role in the liberalization of religion, but it has more generally liberated many religionists in other ways. It has provided them with an occasion for the self-examination that is a necessary condition of significant renewal. It has provided them with a reason to consider the personal and communal relevance of habitual ways of thinking and acting and of the very form of experience and culture to which they profess to be committed. It has invited them to reconsider exactly what it is that they are defending, and why it is worth defending. It has aroused them to confront the corruptions of religion that it has brought into public view, particularly, persistent forms of hatred and hypocrisy. By taking over some of the roles that they and their institutions have traditionally performed in society, television has enabled them to devote themselves more intensively to carrying out religion's loftier cultural roles.

One of the most salutary aspects of fair competition is that it provides sensible, fair-minded competitors with a compelling reason to improve their products and services. Unworthy competitors retreat to force, deception, and defeatism; worthy competitors rise to the challenge. These points apply as much to the most important forms of cultural competition as to the most commonplace kinds of competition in business, sports, and romantic pursuit. With respect to religion itself, as a general rule, religious institutions tend to be morally and spiritually weakest when they are politically most powerful. The greatest glory of religion belongs to its noble martyrs, not to religious leaders who have been successful by worldly standards. Similarly, television has generally been at its best when men and women of inspiration and vision have found projects worth struggling for, projects that challenge the entrenched cultural authorities and the complacent masses. Fair, reasoned criticism of television programming, by religious critics and others, has done only good and no harm. Robert Lee has well observed that, "Surely the cutting edges of a democratic society are at the points of conflict and tension, rather than in those areas where the issues are settled or dormant, where growth is curtailed and social stagnation sets in."[38]

When we reflect at length on the many factors involved in a complex cultural phenomenon like competition between religion and television, we may at times feel overwhelmed by the powerful cultural forces that have so great an influence upon our thought and behavior. We may be all the more discouraged when we consider that these forces may have a far greater influence on the masses of people who are less reflective than we are, or when we consider that competition between religion and television is but one of many such cultural processes taking place. As hard as we may try to avoid a paralyzing determinism, we must be realistic enough to recognize that few individuals are both talented and fortunate enough to be able to exert a great influence on the shape and direction of major cultural processes. Still, we need to remember not only that certain individuals have had a remarkable influence upon the course of civilization, but that most individuals, even many severely disadvantaged ones, have substantial control over the course of their lives as well as significant personal influence on those who are close to them. This is a great existential truth that has sometimes been acknowledged even by cultural anthropologists who have made it their business to explain the power of enculturation. Thus, Ruth Benedict has written that although by the time that he can talk, the individual is already the "little creature of his culture,"[39] it is also true that "no civilization has in it any element which in the last analysis is not the contribution of an individual."[40]

Religious critics of television often speak of the importance of restoring "family values." One of their regular complaints is that television viewing interferes with the interpersonal communication and interaction necessary for wholesome, civilizing family life. When reactionary religionists talk about the need to restore family values and traditional family life, they are sometimes speaking in a coded, rhetorically manipulative language in order to promote their own personal values and attitudes, many of which have little to do with family life as such. Indeed, long before the emergence of the electronic mass media, religious authorities routinely made it their business to interfere with family life, and often the authority that they came to represent was more salutary than any that even well-meaning parents could provide. In any case, whatever the influence of such religious authorities, and whatever the influence of television programmers, loving and devoted parents, and loved ones in general, continue to exert an extremely important form of personal influence on those who trust them and look to them for guidance, encouragement, and emotional support. These people can use television as a tool for meliorating the condition of those whose personal welfare is their primary, fundamental concern; but anyone for whom they are prepared to sacrifice so much can see that television is essentially external to their character and personality, even if it has influenced them in various ways. In contrast, the religious commitment of those whom one looks up to is at the core of their character and personality, so it is not surprising to find even a secular materialist deeply moved when she reports, "My beloved parents, of blessed memory, were good, gentle, godly, religious people," thereby revealing to us some of the impact of having been brought up by people committed to the theological virtues of faith, hope, and love. Of course, many parents, relatives, and teachers are not particularly religious; some are not even especially caring. But generally, on this level of direct personal influence, television cannot compete with religion, and the power of television counts for little or nothing.

It should not be surprising that despite their call for a return to family values and traditional family life, most religious critics of television actually have little confidence in the ability of the typical parents to do the job of civilizing children properly on their own. From the beginnings of civilization, religious and other teachers have had the job, usually freely delegated to them by parents, of educating the young people of the tribe or community in a way that parents themselves have not been able to do. The dissatisfaction of such teachers with the job of civilizing done by most parents is revealed in their criticisms of parents, and has perhaps received its most poignant expression in the strange comments of Jesus that, "I am come to set a man at variance against his father, and the daughter against her mother, and the daughter-in-law against her mother-in-law. And a man's foes *shall be* they of his own household. He that loveth father or mother more than me is not worthy of me: and he that loveth son or daughter more than me is not worthy of me."[41] Yet these were the words of one who professed to be concerned above all with his Father's business[42] and who told his fellow Jews that he honored his Father.[43] However unhappy the earliest Christian teachers may have been with the failings of most parents, they could not ignore the commandment of the Torah, "Honor thy father and thy mother: that thy days may be long upon the land which the Lord thy God giveth thee."[44]

The God of the children of Israel is a personal God—not only the great Master but the great Parent whose everlasting love,[45] though perfect, is to be conceived as comparable to that of those mortals who first nurture the human being and have a special emotional bond with him even after their death. This conception of God has been passed on to Christianity, Islam, and other faiths and worldviews. The idea of such a Being is difficult to conceive, not only because of the negative influence of television, philosophy, and the other cultural rivals of religion, but because it is the natural condition of a reflective human being to find his or her faith in such a Being constantly tested. Many reactionary religionists foolishly believe that wavering faith, loss of faith, and inability to attain faith are evidences of perverse wilfulness, blindness, and weakness when confronted with the agents of darkness. Thoughtful individuals, however, whether already religiously committed or receptive to religious commitment, find themselves challenged in more profound ways.

The greatest challenge to them is the apparently perpetual suffering and inevitable death of human beings, particularly the suffering and death of those dearest to them. Neither television nor philosophy nor awareness of religious hypocrisy has undermined religious faith nearly as much as the failure of traditional theodicy—the inability of the noblest, wisest, and most compassionate of our ancestors and fellows to account for what may well appear to be the arbitrariness, coldness, and impersonality of the forces that determine our destiny. Television programming itself, in both its more obvious and more obscure "religious" forms, does from time to time offer the viewer something in the way of theodicy, and what it offers in this regard is usually derived from the insights of theologians and philosophers. If it does not offer better theodicy than it does, are those who are primarily responsible for television programming to be blamed more than generations of theologians and philosophers? Are indeed any mortals, with their limited understanding, to be blamed for the inadequacy of traditional theodicy in their own minds and the minds of their fellows? And in this age of television, as in ages past, can those who are trying hard to avoid cynicism, pessimism, and fatalism do any better than wait patiently and reverently to be favored, as was Job, with the answer of the Lord delivered "out of the whirlwind"?[46]

NOTES TO CHAPTER 4

1. Neil Postman, *Amusing Ourselves to Death: Public Discourse in the Age of Show Business* (New York: Viking, 1985), p. 92.

2. Steven Starker, *Evil Influences: Crusades against the Mass Media* (New Brunswick, NJ: Transaction Publishers, 1989), p. 7.

3. Cf., for example, Plato *Apology* 23B, 30C–31A, 41C–D.

4. Cf., for example, Plato *Laws* X.

5. Plato *Apology* 18C, 19A–C.

6. Aristophanes, *Clouds*, trans. James H. Mantinband, in James H. Mantinband, *Four Plays of Aristophanes* (Washington: University Press of America, 1983), p. 74.

7. Cf. Jay Newman, *On Religious Freedom* (Ottawa: University of Ottawa Press, 1991), pp. 160–69.

8. Nicolas Berdyaev, *The Fate of Man in the Modern World* (1935), trans. Donald A. Lowrie (Ann Arbor: University of Michigan Press, 1963), p. 114.

9. F. M. Cornford, *From Religion to Philosophy* (1912) (New York: Harper and Brothers, 1957), p. v.

10. Ibid., p. 126.

11. Cf. Newman, *On Religious Freedom*, pp. 169–73.

12. Friedrich Nietzsche, *The Birth of Tragedy* (1872), sec. 23, trans. Francis Golffing (Garden City, NY: Doubleday, 1956), p. 137.

13. Cf. Charles Y. Glock and Rodney Stark, *Religion and Society in Tension* (Chicago: Rand McNally, 1965), pp. 287–306.

14. Plato *Apology* 19D–E.

15. Ibid., 23C–D.

16. Ibid.

17. Ibid., 39C–D.

18. Marshall McLuhan, *Understanding Media: The Extensions of Man* (New York: New American Library, 1964), p. 26.

19. Ibid., p. 34.

20. Ibid., p. 64.

21. Henry J. Perkinson, *Getting Better: Television and Moral Progress* (New Brunswick, NJ: Transaction Publishers, 1991), p. 9.

22. McLuhan, *Understanding Media*, p. 289.

23. Ibid., p. 269.

24. Ibid., p. 270.

25. Ibid., p. 273.

26. Ibid., pp. 268–69, 280–82, 289–92.

27. Ibid., ch. 1–7, p. 31.

28. Plato *Republic* 490C–496E.

29. One cannot do justice in a short space to the genius of the Sophists. An excellent introduction to their achievements is G. B. Kerferd, *The Sophistic Movement* (Cambridge: Cambridge University Press, 1981).

30. McLuhan, *Understanding Media*, pp. 57–58.

31. Postman, *Amusing Ourselves to Death*, pp. 87, 147–48.

32. Michael R. Real, *Mass-Mediated Culture* (Englewood Cliffs, NJ: Prentice-Hall, 1977), p. 270.

33. Newman, *On Religious Freedom*, ch. 2.

34. Ibid., ch. 3.

35. Proverbs 15:33.

36. Micah 6:8.

37. Psalms 138:6.

38. Robert Lee, "Introduction: Religion and Social Conflict," in Robert Lee and Martin Marty, eds., *Religion and Social Conflict* (New York: Oxford University Press, 1964), p. 5.

39. Ruth Benedict, *Patterns of Culture* (Boston: Houghton Mifflin, 1934), p. 3.

40. Ibid., p. 253.

41. Matthew 10:35–37.

42. Luke 2:49.

43. John 8:49.

44. Exodus 20:12.

45. Jeremiah 31:3.

46. Job 38:1, 40:6.

Bibliography

A Public Trust: The Report of the Carnegie Commission on the Future of Public Broad-casting. New York: Bantam Books, 1979.

Abelman, Robert and Stewart M. Hoover, eds. *Religious Television: Controversies and Conclusions*. Norwood, NJ: Ablex, 1990.

Alley, Robert S. *Television: Ethics for Hire?* Nashville: Abingdon, 1977.

Alley, Robert S. "Television and Public Virtue." In John P. Ferré, ed., *Channels of Belief: Religion and American Commercial Television*. Ames: Iowa State University Press, 1990, pp. 45–55.

Andrén, Gunnar. *Media and Morals: The Rationality of Mass Rhetoric and the Autonomy of the Individual*. Stockholm: Akademilitteratur, 1978.

Aristophanes. *Clouds*. Trans. James H. Mantinband. In James H. Mantinband, *Four Plays of Aristophanes*. Washington: University Press of America, 1983.

Bagdikian, Ben H. *The Media Monopoly*. Boston: Beacon Press, 1990 (1983).

Barnouw, Erik. *Tube of Plenty*. New York: Oxford University Press, 1975.

Barr, James. *Fundamentalism*. Philadelphia: Westminster Press, 1977.

Bates, M. Searle. *Religious Liberty: An Inquiry*. New York: Da Capo Press, 1972. (This volume is a reprint of a work first published in 1945 under the auspices of the World Council of Churches.)

Benedict, Ruth. *Patterns of Culture*. Boston: Houghton Mifflin, 1934.

Berdyaev, Nicolas. *The Fate of Man in the Modern World* (1935). Trans. Donald A. Lowrie. Ann Arbor: University of Michigan Press, 1963.

Berger, Arthur Asa. *Television as an Instrument of Terror: Essays on Media, Popular Culture, and Everyday Life*. New Brunswick, NJ: Transaction Books, 1980.

Bill, J. Brent. *Stay Tuned*. Power Books. Old Tappan, NJ: Fleming H. Revell, 1986.

Bird, Roger, ed. *Documents of Canadian Broadcasting*. Ottawa: Carleton University Press, 1988.

Bluem, A. William. *Religious Television Programs: A Study of Relevance*. New York: Hastings House, 1969.

Broughton, Irv. *Producers on Producing*. Jefferson, NC: McFarland, 1986.

Brown, Charles H. *Informing the Public*. New York: Holt, Rinehart and Winston, 1957.

Brown, Les. *Television: The Business Behind the Box*. New York: Harcourt Brace Jovanovich, 1971.

Bruce, Steve. *Pray TV: Televangelism in America*. London: Routledge, 1990.

Buddenbaum, Judith M. "Network News Coverage of Religion." In John P. Ferré, ed., *Channels of Belief: Religion and American Commercial Television*. Ames: Iowa State University Press, 1990, pp. 57–78.

Cantor, Muriel G. *The Hollywood TV Producer: His Work and His Audience*. New Brunswick, NJ: Transaction Books, 1987 (1971).

Carey, James W. *Communication as Culture: Essays on Media and Society*. Boston: Unwin Hyman, 1989.

Cassata, Mary and Thomas Skill. *Television: A Guide to the Literature*. Phoenix: Oryx Press, 1985.

Cassirer, Ernst. *An Essay on Man*. New Haven, CT: Yale University Press, 1944.

Collingwood, R. G. *An Essay on Metaphysics*. Oxford: Clarendon Press, 1940.

Collingwood, R. G. *Speculum Mentis*. Oxford: Clarendon Press, 1924.

Comstock, George. *The Evolution of American Television*. Newbury Park, CA: Sage Publications, 1989.

Cooper, Thomas W., with Robert Sullivan, Christopher Weir, and Peter Medaglia. *Television and Ethics: A Bibliography*. Boston: G. K. Hall, 1988.

Cornford, F. M. *From Religion to Philosophy* (1912). New York: Harper and Brothers, 1957.

Coser, Lewis A. *The Functions of Social Conflict*. Glencoe, IL: Free Press, 1956.

Cox, Harvey. *The Secular City: Secularization and Urbanization in Theological Perspective*, revised ed. New York: Macmillan, 1966 (1965).

Czitrom, Daniel. *Media and the American Mind from Morse to McLuhan*. Chapel Hill: University of North Carolina Press, 1982.

Dawson, Christopher. *Enquiries into Religion and Culture*. New York: Sheed and Ward, 1933.

Dawson, Christopher. *Religion and Culture*. New York: Sheed and Ward, 1948.

Department of Research and Education of the Federal Council of the Churches of Christ in America. *Broadcasting and the Public: A Case Study in Social Ethics*. New York: Abingdon, 1938.

Efron, Edith. *The News Twisters*. Los Angeles: Nash, 1971.

Eliot, T. S. *Notes towards the Definition of Culture*. London: Faber and Faber, 1948.

Ellul, Jacques. *Propaganda: The Formation of Men's Attitudes*. Trans. Konrad Kellen and Jean Lerner. New York: Alfred A. Knopf, 1968.

Englebert, Omer. *The Lives of the Saints*. Trans. Christopher and Anne Fremantle. New York: Collier Books, 1964.

Evans, Donald. *Struggle and Fulfilment: The Inner Dynamics of Religion and Morality*. London: Collins, 1979.

Fackre, Gabriel. *The Religious Right and Christian Faith*. Grand Rapids, MI: William B. Eerdmans, 1982.

Ferré, John P., ed. *Channels of Belief: Religion and American Commercial Television*. Ames: Iowa State University Press, 1990.

Fore, William F. *Television and Religion: The Shaping of Faith, Values, and Culture.* Minneapolis: Augsburg, 1987.

Fowles, Jib. *Television Viewers vs. Media Snobs: What TV Does for People.* New York: Stein and Day, 1982.

Frankl, Razelle. *Televangelism: The Marketing of Popular Religion.* Carbondale: Southern Illinois University Press, 1987.

Freud, Sigmund. *The Future of an Illusion* (1927). Trans. W. D. Robson-Scott (1953), revised and newly ed. James Strachey (1961). Garden City, NY: Doubleday, 1964.

Gans, Herbert J. *Deciding What's News: A Study of* CBS Evening News, NBC Nightly News, Newsweek, *and* Time. New York: Pantheon Books, 1979.

Gerbner, George. "Television: The New State Religion?" *ETC.*, 34, 2 (June 1977), pp. 145–50.

Glick, Ira O. and Sidney J. Levy. *Living with Television.* Chicago: Aldine, 1962.

Glock, Charles Y. and Rodney Stark. *Religion and Society in Tension.* Chicago: Rand McNally, 1965.

Goethals, Gregor T. *The TV Ritual: Worship at the Video Altar.* Boston: Beacon Press, 1980.

Gray, John. *Liberalism.* Milton Keynes, England: Open University Press, 1986.

Hadden, Jeffery K. and Charles E. Swann. *Prime Time Preachers: The Rising Power of Televangelism.* Reading, MA: Addison-Wesley, 1981.

Head, Sydney W. and Christopher H. Sterling. *Broadcasting in America.* Boston: Houghton Mifflin, 1987 (1956).

Hick, John. *God and the Universe of Faiths.* London: Macmillan, 1973.

Hill, George H. and Lenwood Davis. *Religious Broadcasting: An Annotated Bibliography.* New York: Garland, 1984.

Hook, Sidney. *Religion in a Free Society.* Lincoln: University of Nebraska Press, 1967.

Hoover, Stewart M. *The Electronic Giant: A Critique of the Telecommunications Revolution from a Christian Perspective.* Elgin, IL: The Brethren Press, 1982.

Hoover, Stewart M. *Mass Media Religion: The Social Sources of the Electronic Church.* Newbury Park, CA: Sage Publications, 1988.

Horsfield, Peter G. *Religious Television: The American Experience.* New York: Longmans, 1984.

Howitt, Dennis. *The Mass Media and Social Problems.* Oxford: Pergamon, 1982.

Innis, Harold A. *The Bias of Communication.* Toronto: University of Toronto Press, 1951.

James, William. *The Varieties of Religious Experience.* New York: Longmans, Green, 1902.

Kerferd, G. B. *The Sophistic Movement.* Cambridge: Cambridge University Press, 1981.

Kuhns, William. *The Electronic Gospel: Religion and the Media.* New York: Herder and Herder, 1969.

Lawhead, Stephen R. *Turn Back the Night.* Westchester, IL: Crossway Books, 1985.

Lee, Robert and Martin Marty, eds. *Religion and Social Conflict.* New York: Oxford University Press, 1964.

Lemert, James B. *Criticizing the Media: Empirical Approaches.* Newbury Park, CA: Sage Publications, 1989.

Levinson, Richard and William Link. *Stay Tuned*. New York: St. Martin's, 1981.

Lichter, S. Robert, Stanley Rothman, and Linda S. Lichter. *The Media Elite*. Bethesda, MD: Adler and Adler, 1986.

Lippmann, Walter. *A Preface to Morals*. New York: Macmillan, 1929.

Lippmann, Walter. *Public Opinion*. New York: Macmillan, 1922.

Mander, Jerry. *Four Arguments for the Elimination of Television*. New York: Quill, 1978.

Manzullo, Donald A. *Neither Sacred nor Profane*. New York: Exposition Press, 1973.

McLuhan, Marshall. *Understanding Media: The Extensions of Man*. New York: New American Library, 1964.

Mendelsohn, Harold. *Mass Entertainment*. New Haven, CT: College and University Press, 1966.

Miller, Donald E. *The Case for Liberal Christianity*. San Francisco: Harper and Row, 1981.

Muller, Herbert J. *Issues of Freedom: Paradoxes and Promises*. New York: Harper and Brothers, 1960.

Nelson, Joyce. *The Perfect Machine: TV in the Nuclear Age*. Toronto: Between the Lines, 1987.

Neusner, Jacob. *Jews and Christians: The Myth of a Common Tradition*. London: SCM Press, 1991.

Newcomb, Horace, ed. *Television: The Critical View*. New York: Oxford University Press, 1994 (1976).

Newcomb, Horace and Robert S. Alley. *The Producer's Medium: Conversations with Creators of American TV*. New York: Oxford University Press, 1983.

Newman, Jay. *Competition in Religious Life*. Editions SR, Vol. 11. Waterloo, ON: Wilfrid Laurier University Press, 1989.

Newman, Jay. *Fanatics and Hypocrites*. Buffalo, NY: Prometheus Books, 1986.

Newman, Jay. *Foundations of Religious Tolerance*. Toronto: University of Toronto Press, 1982.

Newman, Jay. *The Journalist in Plato's Cave*. Rutherford, NJ: Fairleigh Dickinson University Press; London and Toronto: Associated University Presses, 1989.

Newman, Jay. *On Religious Freedom*. Ottawa: University of Ottawa Press, 1991.

Nietzsche, Friedrich. *The Anti-Christ* (1895; written in 1888). Trans. R. J. Hollingdale. London: Penguin Books, 1990 (1968).

Nietzsche, Friedrich. *Beyond Good and Evil* (1886). Trans. Walter Kaufmann. New York: Vintage Books, 1966.

Nietzsche, Friedrich. *The Birth of Tragedy* (1872). Trans. Francis Golffing. Garden City, NY: Doubleday, 1956.

Perkinson, Henry J. *Getting Better: Television and Moral Progress*. New Brunswick, NJ: Transaction Publishers, 1991.

Phelan, John M. *Disenchantment: Meaning and Morality in the Media*. New York: Hastings House, 1980.

Plato. *Apology*.

Plato. *Laws*.

Plato. *Republic*.

Porter, David. *The Media: A Christian Point of View*. London: Scripture Union, 1974.

Postman, Neil. *Amusing Ourselves to Death: Public Discourse in the Age of Show Business*. New York: Viking, 1985.

Postman, Neil. *The Disappearance of Childhood*. New York: Delacorte Press, 1982.

Real, Michael R. *Mass-Mediated Culture*. Englewood Cliffs, NJ: Prentice-Hall, 1977.

Russell, Bertrand. *Religion and Science*. London: Oxford University Press, 1961.

Schiller, Herbert I. *Culture, Inc.: The Corporate Takeover of Public Expression*. New York: Oxford University Press, 1989.

Schiller, Herbert I. *Mass Communications and American Empire*. Boston: Beacon Press, 1971.

Schramm, Wilbur. *Responsibility in Mass Communication*. New York: Harper and Row, 1957.

Schultze, Quentin J. *Televangelism and American Culture: The Business of Popular Religion*. Grand Rapids, MI: Baker Book House, 1991.

Schultze, Quentin J. *Television: Manna from Hollywood?* Grand Rapids, MI: Zondervan, 1986.

Schultze, Quentin J. "Television Drama as a Sacred Text." In John P. Ferré, ed., *Channels of Belief: Religion and American Commercial Television*. Ames: Iowa State University Press, 1990, pp. 3–27.

Schütz, John Howard. *Paul and the Anatomy of Apostolic Authority*. Cambridge: Cambridge University Press, 1975.

Schwartz, Tony. *Media: The Second God*. New York: Random House, 1981.

Seiden, Martin H. *Access to the American Mind: The Impact of the New Mass Media*. New York: Shapolsky, 1991.

Shanks, Bob. *The Cool Fire*. New York: W. W. Norton, 1976.

Shapiro, J. Salwyn. *Liberalism: Its Meaning and History*. Princeton, NJ: D. Van Nostrand, 1958.

Sherman, Barry L. *Telecommunications Management: The Broadcast & Cable Industries*. New York: McGraw-Hill, 1987.

Slusher, Howard S. *Man, Sport and Existence: A Critical Analysis*. Philadelphia: Lea and Febiger, 1967.

Sobel, Lester A., ed. *Media Controversies*. New York: Facts on File Inc., 1981.

Sobel, Robert. *The Manipulators: America in the Media Age*. Garden City, NY: Anchor Press, 1976.

Starker, Steven. *Evil Influences: Crusades against the Mass Media*. New Brunswick, NJ: Transaction Publishers, 1989.

Steiner, Gary A. *The People Look at Television*. New York: Alfred A. Knopf, 1963.

Sterling, Christopher H. and John M. Kittross. *Stay Tuned: A Concise History of American Broadcasting*. Belmont, CA: Wadsworth, 1990 (1978).

Twitchell, James B. *Carnival Culture: The Trashing of Taste in America*. New York: Columbia University Press, 1992.

Whitehouse, Mary. *Cleaning-Up TV: From Protest to Participation*. London: Blandford Press, 1967.

Wildmon, Donald E. *The Home Invaders*. Wheaton, IL: SP Publications, 1985.

Winn, Marie. *The Plug-in Drug: Television, Children, and the Family*. New York: Grossman, 1977.

Wober, J. Mallory. *The Use and Abuse of Television: A Social Psychological Analysis of the Changing Screen*. Hillsdale, NJ: Lawrence Erlbaum Associates, 1988.

Wurtzel, Alan and Stephen R. Acker. *Television Production*. New York: McGraw-Hill, 1989 (1979).

Zolf, Dorothy and Paul W. Taylor. "Redressing the Balance in Canadian Broadcasting: A History of Religious Broadcasting Policy in Canada." *Studies in Religion/Sciences Religieuses*, 18, 2 (1989), pp. 153–70.

Index

About the Author

JAY NEWMAN is Professor of Philosophy at the University of Guelph. He is a Fellow of the Royal Society of Canada and a past president of the Canadian Theological Society. He is the author of *Foundations of Religious Tolerance* (1982), *Fanatics and Hypocrites* (1986), *Competition in Religious Life* (1989), *The Journalist in Plato's Cave* (1989), and *On Religious Freedom* (1991). His numerous articles have appeared in such journals as *Philosophy*, *Ethics*, and *Religious Studies*.